music
through the
renaissance

The Brown Music Horizons Series

[music through the renaissance]

James C. Thomson
West Chester State College

WM. C. BROWN COMPANY PUBLISHERS, *Dubuque, Iowa*

The tremendous growth and interest in basic music appreciation and literature courses and the increasing emphasis on music for the general college student demands fresh approaches to teaching and learning at the introductory level. The Music Horizons Series represents a significant attempt to meet these needs by providing students with stimulating material of high quality by an authority in the field as well as providing instructors with the advantage of complete flexibility in organizing and teaching their course. Although the individual titles are self-contained, collectively they cover the full scope of music appreciation, literature and history.

TO

MY FAMILY

preface

"But everyone knows there was no music before 1700!"

This aggressively and abysmally ignorant statement was made thirty years ago by a professor of physics to the harpsichordist Eta Harich-Schneider, who related it to me. She had told the professor her repertoire included music written in England about 1600.

Such a lamentable state of affairs is not so difficult to understand when one considers that a generation ago recordings and performances of early music were extremely rare. Furthermore, some discs were made under poor technical conditions by insensitive performers.

Thus it is surprising that during the winter of 1949-50 it was possible for a New Haven electronics engineer, also a music enthusiast, to own enough recordings to plan, annotate, and announce a series of thirty one-hour programs of Medieval and Renaissance music for a local FM station. I recorded the whole series on tape — but as the years have rolled by these tapes have been gathering more and more dust.

One reason for the neglect is that high-fidelity recording has been perfected and audio itself is now a fine art. Moreover, music by composers of the Middle Ages and the Renaissance is now available in greater quantity. Best of all, recordings are now made by musicians of high ability and standing, and there is a steady increase in the number of professional music groups organized for the purpose of performing early music and recording it. Their warmth and fervor, along with fine scholarship, convince the listener there is real enjoyment in what they are doing. Amateurs, too, are continuously finding new delight in singing and playing music from older repertories, often on replicas of ancient instruments. In short, more people are aware that Medieval and Renaissance music is no longer like Pheasant under Glass — something people hear about but seldom come to enjoy.

This book is primarily intended to introduce the general college student to music before 1600. References are made to specific examples and recordings. They direct the reader to compositions discussed or mentioned in the preceding passages and to other works by the same composer(s). They may be used as listening and study assignments to supplement those provided after each chapter. The independent reader, not enrolled in any music course, will find these references especially helpful. A list of sources for further reading forms a basis for additional study.

As a convenient tool in the customary use of recordings, the list in the Appendix will prove serviceable to both the individual reader and teacher. The author recommends that the reader have access to the first volume of Davison and Apel's *Historical Anthology of Music.* Other anthologies listed in the bibliography are also extremely valuable. Books mentioned in the introductory paragraph to the bibliography provide lists of collections and other basic material.

I am especially grateful to my good friends, Dr. and Mrs. J. Bunker Clark and Dr. Jack B. Oruch, and my wife, for reading the manuscript and making suggestions. I am indebted to Monsieur R. Bragard at the Museum of Musical Instruments in Brussels for his help in supplying photographs. My thanks are due also to Miss Joyce Bridgman for proofreading the typescript.

James C. Thomson

July 25, 1966

contents

primitive music

Some holiday wanderers through the forest are content, when they find a swift brook, to admire its beauty and drink of its clear abundance. After resting, they cross and continue on their way. More curious travelers, before going on, may feel impelled to glance upstream and wonder where its source may be.

We cannot look back to see the beginning of man's time; no more can we listen back to hear the beginning of man's music. The stream of time, the course of music, and the life of man are nearly one, for he probably had music soon after he learned to speak.

Those many people who have wondered how music originated have proposed a number of theories: men learned music by imitating animals, while courting the opposite sex, while working together to make teamwork more pleasurable, or by employing an impassioned or intensified speech. The Greeks of antiquity were satisfied to assign the invention of music to singer-poets long dead and to their gods. Specialists today believe speech and music arose from a common background as a combined, unintelligible form of precommunication. Both had pitch, stress, duration — both developed simultaneously.

ARCHAEOLOGY

In our curiosity to explore the past there are two methods we can follow. The first may be called vertical — we can dig. We restore many artifacts from the darkness of the earth to the eyes of man, and archaeology can tell us approximately when these were created. For sculpture, a vase, or a cylix, this method may be fully satisfying — an object of art may stand before us and be enjoyed in its entirety much as it was when new.

From representations on vases and other treasures of the visual arts we see people playing and singing and we learn how music was used. We find out about their instruments and discover their systems of notation. But the ultimate experience of music is beyond reach, we cannot hear how the music sounded — listen as we may, no melodies of the past ever come from a hole in the ground.

CONTEMPORARY PRIMITIVE TRIBES

Though the actual sound of music in history has vanished forever, we learn more about man's earliest music by turning to the second method: the horizontal — we raise our eyes and look about us. There are tribes of primitive people alive today whose cultures go back as far as the stone age. Comparatively little touched by centuries of change, their agriculture, hunting, traditions, art, dances, and music are much the same as they were thousands of years ago. These people, though they have a tribal organization, possess no writing system. When we speak of primitive music we refer to the music of preliterate societies such as these.

Their Music

With no system of written records, primitive tribes sometimes depend on strict methods to preserve elements of their culture they tenaciously believe must not be forgotten or altered. Their music is transmitted by oral tradition. Yet the music of most contemporary primitive men is not necessarily the same as that of their ancestors, for it has come a long way from prehistoric music. Most primitives of today have learned through contact with other tribes, and in cases where warlike tribes have overcome less aggressive ones the vanquished have been forced to accept traditions of the conqueror. Only when we encounter a primitive tribe in a remote valley, isolated from other tribes for centuries, may we look to their heritage as a guide to our knowledge of man's earliest music. Most primitive music of the twentieth century is not the essence but the echo of prehistory.

melodic styles

It seems certain that music began with singing and dancing. Today's most primitive people, such as the Vedda of Ceylon, have no instruments. They and the Botocudos of Brazil sing in tone groupings that could hardly be called scales. Their melodies are of two tones, usually a major second apart, though in primitive music it is difficult to determine the size of intervals with accuracy because they may vary from one performance to another. One-step music is often merely a vehicle

Example 1.   Primitive chanting on notes a major second apart.

WerW, p. 308.

SaRi, p. 32.

for a text. It is unemotional and usually sung with little or no emphasis. Two-note melodies also occur in which the interval is a minor second, a third, a fourth, or a fifth.

Another type of primitive music arises out of a burst of passion which suggests joy, rage, ecstasy, or tension. Beginning on a high pitch torn from the singer's throat with violence, the melody cascades in a descending torrent with gradually decreasing intensity until, with the singer out of breath, the pitch is at its lowest point. There are many repetitions. Sometimes these cascading melodies have no fixed landing points of pitch in their haphazard descent; other tribes spread their melodies over an octave and recognizable intervals appear. Tribes in the Torres Straits, the Kubu in Sumatra, and some in various parts of Australia are associated with this type of singing.

Between these two extremes (the undulating, expressionless, one-step, and descending, ecstatic, wide-range) appear infinite varieties and combinations. Where actual scales are recognizable, a pentatonic scale with no half-steps — for example, the various patterns of pitches obtained from sounding the black keys on the piano — is widespread. Scales with four, six, or seven tones usually resemble our diatonic scale. In music of cultured parts of the orient an octave may contain as many as twenty-two or more different pitches.

other characteristics

Simple cultures are content with simple rhythms. The Vedda, for example, have no solo drums, no solo percussive music. In contrast, some highly organized cultures can boast of rhythms more complex than any in Western music. Isorhythm, which makes use of a repeated rhythmic pattern (cf. p. 58f), and rhythmic polyphony have astounded Western listeners.

When songs are short, they may be through-composed, the melody being newly created as it progresses. Longer ones may be strophic, the most common form. But many examples resemble a litany, and with hundreds of repetitions of short particles may go on for hours.

Nearly all primitive cultures combine voices at different pitch levels in some elementary way. Consonances commonly occur when men and women anywhere sing the same melody together. But in many groups in various parts of the world some singers, in full belief that they are on pitch with the others, sing the melody a fifth or fourth above or below. Parallel fifths or fourths are the result, to be compared with medieval part writing in Western Europe (see Chapter 3). Parallel thirds are sung by Bantu Africans and native Micronesians on the Caroline Islands. Most astounding are parallel seconds heard among certain Polynesians and several other tribes. In cases of more-than-one-line music the singing is done by groups, not soloists, and the two voices consist of essentially the same melody, even though there are decorations, at different pitch levels.

music in tribal life

In primitive music, participation is general — all members know and sing tribal songs. Thus, music is usually on an amateur basis. A new song is accepted into tribal repertoire only after it has been approved by the whole group. It may come from a dream, or while a man is building a boat. He works on his new song by singing it over many times — the composer cannot write it down and must therefore learn and polish his new creation through repetition. Only when he feels it is perfect does he dare present it to the tribe; not unless it finds favor with the community does the song become part of tribal tradition.

While music performed in Western concert halls is usually a result of some composer's aim to create a work of beauty, the primitive has little regard for this. To him only functional qualities are of any real significance; music must serve a useful purpose — it must be practical. Dancing, whether part of the religious ritual or of secular occasions, is inseparable from its music. Love songs, story telling, the rallying of warriors to battle, signaling over distances — for all these the music is functional.

In short, to primitive man music is magic. In religious rites, music invokes powers of good spirits and frightens away evil ones. In dances it may be part of a charm to bring rain or a bountiful harvest. A love song is supposed to render the loved one incapable of resistance. An enemy is to be destroyed through the sorcery of incantation. In situations over which the primitive has no control he relies on magic, the supernatural, to bring about what he desires. To him, music is the best means to call on forces of good or evil.

Musical Instruments

In the course of magic rituals the primitive may attempt to attract spirits by disguising his natural voice. If he holds a drum before his mouth his voice becomes mysterious, even supranatural. To attract rain his cries will surely be more effective if he projects them into the shell of some water animal. The rattle is an amulet with magic power; the flute is a symbol of fertility and rebirth. Some of man's early musical instruments arose out of his attempts to move the supernatural.

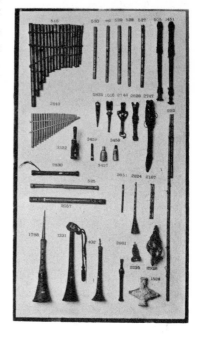

But even as he sang his first songs man became conscious of the rhythm that grew out of the ritualistic expression of his emotions. It was second nature to reinforce rhythm with motions of the body such as slapping his hands against his sides, clapping them together, and stamping on the ground. And, just as he had discovered that a club was more efficient than his bare hands against an enemy, he also found he could make his dancing more forceful if he filled a gourd with pebbles or strung rattles in bunches and attached them to his feet, his knees, his neck. Every implement, every tool man has ever used is in some way

Figure 1. African instruments: pan pipes, flutes of many kinds, rattles, double reeds. (Courtesy of the Metropolitan Museum of Art, Crosby Brown Collection of Musical Instruments, 1889.)

an extension of some part of his body. So, too, are musical instruments. The sound of the stamping foot was increased when the dancer stood on some form of plank; even this was improved if the plank or a hollowed-out tree lay across a pit in the ground. A longitudinal slit cut into the tree turned it into the now common slit drum.

Rattles, bone flutes, and bull roarers (a narrow board, sometimes in the shape of a fish, whirled on the end of a string) have been dug up in earth strata deposited in the stone age. The musical bow, too, is very ancient. One was painted on the wall of a cave about seventeen thousand years ago. Unlike our modern bow, used as a mute accessory to coax music from a member of the violin family, this is an instrument in itself, producing its own melodies — the twang of the bowstring can be raised or lowered in pitch by varying tension on the string. A gourd is sometimes attached to the stick, or the bow may be grasped in the teeth so the mouth acts as a resonator. This is probably an ancestor, through single-string fiddles and lutes, of more complicated instruments like zithers and harps. The musical bow is associated with women as players, or with feminine rites. Nearly every instrument with any kind of resonating cavity is feminine; the flute and all similarly shaped instruments are phallic: to the primitive, all instruments have sexual connotations.

Figure 2. Stopped pipes of West Coast North American Indians. A central block is grooved on six sides, to which outside pieces are cemented and bound with cord. (Courtesy of the Metropolitan Museum of Art, Crosby Brown Collection of Musical Instruments, 1889.)

ETHNOMUSICOLOGY

The science concerned with all phases of music outside our own Western culture is called ethnomusicology. In the 1880s pioneering efforts were made by Carl Stumpf and Erich von Hornbostel, psychologists at the University of Berlin, who were interested in primitive scales, intervals, and tone systems. The invention of the phonograph only a few years before (1876) was the greatest single aid to the ethnomusicologist. Now he could carry actual sounds back to his laboratory and analyze them. Further precision in measurement was provided about the same time (1884) through the ingenuity of an Englishman, A. J. Ellis, whose interests included spelling reform, phonetics, and acoustics. Totally tone-deaf, he relied on mathematics and devised a system whereby each tempered semitone is divided into a hundred equal parts called cents.

In the United States early researchers were anthropologists and practicing musicians. The first recordings of primitive music, performed by Passamaquoddy and Zuñi Indians, were made by Dr. Walter Fewkes in 1889 and analyzed by Dr. B. I. Gilman of Harvard. Phonographic archives increased with amazing rapidity, for it was soon realized that primitive music in its native surroundings would fast dissappear. (Until three hundred years ago all music in the western hemisphere was primitive.) Ethnomusicology has now developed into a precise, complex science. Workers must have devoted long, thorough study to the cultures of people whose music they wish to record. They must know how to find out who important singers are; they must gain their confidence and ascertain how melodies are used and in which context they are employed. Laboratory techniques in transcribing unusual intervals, pitches, and rhythms are very accurate. Through ethnomusicology and by means of the tape recorder, the long-playing record, and other electronic instruments, amateurs and scientists now have available many examples of primitive music from all over the world.

SOURCES AND ADDITIONAL READINGS*

EaH	NeT	SaWH
KuE	SaH	SchnO
NeM	SaRi	WerW
	SaWe	

QUESTIONS ON THE TEXT

1. What principal theories have been proposed in the past regarding the origin of music? What is the current belief about how music began?
2. What can we find out about music of the past through archaeological methods? In what way is this method unsatisfing? How may we learn more about man's earliest music?

---

*The key to symbols and full references are given in the Bibliography.

3. Under what circumstances may we accept primitive music as closely resembling prehistoric music?
4. Discuss two contrasting types of primitive music.
5. What have you learned about rhythms and forms of primitive music? Explain the nature of primitive singing at more than one pitch level.
6. What is the importance of music in primitive life? Who are the performers?
7. How did primitive instruments originate? How are they used? What are some of the earliest ones?
8. What is ethnomusicology? How does it achieve its results?

ASSIGNMENTS

1. Listen to Folkways FE 4431, side 1, band 3; FE 4439, side 2, band 3; and FE 4428, side 1, band 3. How would you classify the music sung in these examples?
2. Listen to Folkways FE 4525 (2 discs): *Man's Early Musical Instruments* (foot stamping, tapping sticks, rattles, scrapers, slit-drums, pipe and tabor, pan pipes, nose flute, etc.).

music in ancient greece

• All nations have had traditional stories, varying in scope and quantity. As children we heard many Greek myths and even as grownups we admire the imaginative power of their creators. Myths help make the primeval past of a nation understandable to the ordinary person; when based on actual events, they draw the past into the present. Whether containing a grain of truth or not, their accounts live on as though their past had been actual history.

In ancient Greece the people who sang and even spun these tales were the singer-poets. Not having a priestly hierarchy, the Greeks assigned a prominent position to the singer-poet, who exemplified unity between music and poetry, an essential quality of the artistic life not only of Greek antiquity but of more primitive people as well. Often the Greeks deified famous singer-poets of the distant past. The gods themselves, they believed, were always singing, and even invented some of their instruments. According to legend, Hermes created the lyre, Apollo the kithara, Pan the pipes.

MUSICAL INSTRUMENTS

Although we usually hear more about the aulos, lyre, and kithara, the Greeks actually had quite a variety of instruments. Several terms refer to varieties of the harp. Trumpets were used for many kinds of public celebrations but principally for war, when their main purpose was to frighten the enemy. One Greek trumpet still preserved has a bronze bell; the main part of the tube consists of ivory with thirteen joints each covered with a bronze ring. Percussion instruments, used primarily in the worship of Dionysus and Cybele, were generally played by women. There were hand-beaten frame drums, clappers (frequently part of the sandal of a chorus leader), large and small cymbals, tambourines, and rattles.

The Aulos

However, melody-playing instruments were better suited to the nature of Greek music. The aulos (pl. *auloi*) was *not* a flute as still mistakenly described even in very recent books on Greek art and culture. Sound was produced usually by means of a double reed; hence, the aulos is more related to the oboe. The tube, made of cane, wood, bone, or ivory, was cylindrical and overblew at the interval of a twelfth, the total range being about two and a half octaves. Three or four equally spaced holes in early instruments were later increased to as many as fifteen, in which case collars were provided to cover holes not being used. A bulb or series of bulbs often depicted at the top of the instrument probably covered the stalk of the reeds, which were inserted all the way into the mouth. Often a strap around the cheeks and head

Figure 3. Greek krater, about 440 B.C. Man playing **auloi.** (Courtesy of the Metropolitan Museum of Art, Rogers Fund, 1921.)

helped maintain wind pressure so the tone could be sustained continuously, like that of the bagpipe, without being interrupted for breathing. *Auloi* were usually employed in pairs, in which case one of the tubes may have been a drone.

The aulos was associated with the worship of Dionysus, hence very significant in accompanying the drama. Five different sizes, intended for different functions, are believed to have been in use.

The Lyre

According to legend, Hermes, son of Zeus, found an empty tortoise shell with dried sinews strung across it and presented it to Apollo who made from it the first lyre. Fastened to and extending from the shell were two animal horns or slender pieces of wood. From a crossbar at their extreme ends strings extended back across the body of the instrument. These were on the same plane[1] as a piece of animal skin acting

Figure 4. Greek amphora, fifth century B.C. Apollo and Artemis before an altar. Apollo is playing a lyre (note plectrum in his right hand). (Courtesy of the Metropolitan Museum of Art, Rogers Fund, 1907.)

as a soundboard that covered the opening of the shell. A bridge supported the strings on the animal skin. The earliest instruments had only three or four strings, but there may have been as many as twelve in the fifth century B.C.

The lyre was a folk instrument primarily for beginners and amateurs. It was played usually in a horizontal position and served mostly to accompany singers.

The Kithara

By contrast, the kithara was the instrument of the advanced amateur or professional and was played in an upright position. Made of wood, it was longer and heavier than the lyre. Virtuosos used it for solos as well as accompaniments. The fingers of the right hand, or preferably a plectrum, swept across all strings of the lyre or kithara, certain of which were deadened by fingers of the left hand; strings remaining free pro-

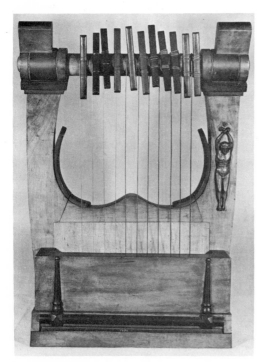

Figure 5. Reproduction of a kithara (model in the Vatican Museum). (Courtesy of Instrument Museum, Brussels.)

duced the pitches desired. Both instruments were tuned to a pentatonic scale without semitones. The fingers of the left hand could also be used to raise the pitches of the strings. Written music for the lyre and kithara was actually a tablature showing where the fingers were to be placed.

Both instruments were in use in Greece by 1000 B.C., though the kithara was known in Sumeria about 2800 B.C.

THE SINGER-POET

The kithara, associated with the worship of Apollo, was the instrument of the singer-poet. Orpheus, one of the singer-poets who became deified, was said to have been the son of Apollo and Calliope. He may have been an actual person. Magic attributed to his music reached into the impossible: it was claimed he could cast a spell on all of nature, that he invented poetic hexameter and even the alphabet itself.

Linus was another singer-poet, the teacher of Hercules who killed him in a fit of anger. To Marsyas, another mythical figure, was attributed the invention of the aulos. Thamyris, a legendary musician mentioned in the *Iliad*, was blinded by the muses, who punished many a singer-poet who became too vain or so famed that the muses were jealous.

MUSIC IN RELIGION

The Greeks were very imaginative in creating gods as well as myths. In their polytheism there was no dogma; thus, there was no need for a priesthood as an intermediary between the gods and man. Sacrifices could be performed at home by the head of the family. Their priests were merely functionaries, servants of the temples of the gods. Larger temples also had musicians who accompanied important rites, and much money was sometimes spent for large choirs and groups of aulos players. The Greek religion was the responsibility of the city-state, which made sure the gods were treated with respect and their rites faithfully observed.

Religious rites could not take place without music. Even when celebrated in the home a paean was sung after each meal following a sacrifice. For public sacrifices huge choirs with aulos and kithara players had places in tremendous processions together with the officers of the temple, guardsmen, and the animals to be sacrificed. Hymns and paeans were dedicated to the particular god being venerated. The ritual was divided into two parts, a preliminary ceremony and the sacrifice proper during which prayers were said to special musical formulas, supplemented by music on the aulos. Thus, music was a part of the sacrificial act, not just a decoration. Paeans and hymns were sung after the conclusion of the ritual too, during the feast that followed the sacrifice.

Every god, temple, and city-state had its fundamental melodies which remained fixed and unchanged, although they might be varied during performance. Such a melody was called a nome (*nomos*, pl. *nomoi*). A nome might be associated with a particular god or goddess (Nome of Athena), medium (purely sung or sung and accompanied by the kithara or aulos), poetic meter (iambic nome), or form (sectional). Sakádos in 586 B.C. wrote a sectional nome for the aulos, telling the story of Apollo's fight with a dragon — the first known example of program music.

MUSIC IN GREEK LIFE

The city-state also supervised musical instruction. Citizens received training until they were thirty years old. Children were taught to sing paeans and hymns to the gods and to national heroes. Adults might be expected to sing on social or religious occasions. No one could claim he didn't know how because for a long time musical training was universal. At first, choirs at religious sacrifices were not professional — any citizen could be a member. Eventually professional choirs did arise; we are told they existed by the fourth century B.C. They trained for all kinds of religious services, achieving virtuosity and national fame. Appointments to these choirs were made on the basis of skill so they no longer represented the citizens at large. Choirs thus became smaller yet more expensive and luxurious to maintain, the members more pampered and temperamental. With less incentive for the individual, universal training languished. With the decline in resources of city-states, the expensive choirs vanished and elaborate public sacrifices had to be abandoned. By the end of the second century B.C. public festivals died out and rites of the cult were returned to the private home.

Individuals had opportunities to perform in contests, called agons, taking place after religious festivals. Pindar of Thebes (c.522-433 B.C.) was famous for his odes, as was also Sappho, who lived in the late seventh and early sixth centuries B.C. A native of the island of Lesbos, she had a school of poetry and music for women there. She was slightly preceded by Terpander of the seventh century B.C., one of the first definite figures in Greek music, and also one of the singer-poets later deified in myths. He had a school for singers and kithara players on the same island, training young men for musical participation in religious services and agons and writing *nomoi* for voice and instruments. He was subsequently called to Sparta to help calm political conditions by means of his music.

The Doctrine of the Ethos

The Greeks believed music could exert a tremendous power over the mind and soul of man. They believed ecstasy, physical frenzy, or intoxicating passion could be aroused by listening to music played on the aulos. They also believed that other kinds of music could restore the soul from a state of confusion to one of calm, disciplined control. A melody lying high within a natural range was considered exciting, a low one more soothing. Any state of mind that was an aberration could be brought back to normal by listening to the kind of music having the desired healing effect. This was called *catharsis*. Plato and Aristotle tell us that a very important factor in the effect any melody might have on the human mind or soul was the mode in which it was written. The Dorian mode was considered sedate and manly, thus being good for improving the state of the soul; the Phrygian stirred men to a state of enthusiasm that was also purifying. The Lydian was soft, convivial, relaxed. Also of significance was the rhythm of the music, which had to follow the rhythm of the words. Thus, the effect of a piece of music depended on its range, mode, rhythm, and text. Aristotle believed that in order to achieve a well-adjusted personality a young person should have an education based on a proper balance between musical and physical training.

Science and Philosophy

The Greeks developed doctrines leading to the science of acoustics. In the sixth century B.C. Pythagoras experimented with a vibrating string and discovered the exact numerical ratios of musical intervals. The Greeks believed that number ruled the entire universe: the motions of celestial bodies, the orbits of stars. Pythagoras and his followers considered that the earth was a globe and that the sun, while circulating around the earth, was the center of the revolutions of Venus and Mercury. They observed that all motion produces sound. They theorized that number governed motions of the planets and other heavenly bodies and that numerical relationships between their orbits, their distances from the central luminary, were like numerical ratios between notes of musical intervals. Thus, there must be harmonic proportions in the cosmos: stars and planets in their orbits must be producing incessant harmony, a music of the spheres, later given the Latin term *musica mundana*. Furthermore, they observed that men's lives moved in certain rhythms; this regularity, too, was possible only through proportions of numbers. This balance in men's lives has been called *musica humana*.

The Greeks believed that *musica mundana* and *musica humana* were not audible to men much in the same way that people cease to be aware of a sound they constantly hear and thus are unable to compare with silence. All forms of music, both vocal and instrumental, that were audible to mankind were included in the term *musica instrumentalis*.

This attempt to explain the universe in musical terms was taken into the Greek teaching of philosophy. Music became a branch of philosophy, eventually to be counted among the seven liberal arts.

RELICS OF GREEK MUSIC

There remain very few actual relics in Greek notation; about a dozen examples are known. These include fragments of music from the drama; hymns to Apollo and the muses; a little instrumental music; and a drinking song, a *skolion* written by Seikilos to the memory of his wife Euterpe, and found engraved on a column in Asia Minor. Most of these relics are from the first and second centuries B.C. An exception is the music of the Oxyrhynchos papyrus, actually part of a Christian hymn in Greek notation from the third century A.D. (HAM, No. 7; Omn, p. 1; GlE, p. 1.)

Greek ideas on music were transmitted to the Middle Ages in the treatises of Boethius, Cassiodorus, and others (cf. p. 32), and thus influenced philosophy and science almost until the middle of the seventeenth century. In music as well as in other disciplines the Greeks were teachers of the Western world.

SOURCES AND ADDITIONAL READINGS

BesA	KiP	SaH
BuI	MarD	SaRi
GrB	MilG	SchlG
GuthG	MirD	StrS
	ReMMA	

QUESTIONS ON THE TEXT

1. What was the significance of the myth to the Greeks?
2. What instruments did the Greeks have? Which was a double-reed instrument? How was it used?
3. What were the differences between the lyre and the kithara? How were they played? How were they used?
4. What role was filled by the singer-poet? Discuss some of them and their mythical accomplishments.

5. How did the Greeks use music in their religion?
6. In what ways did the Greeks believe music might affect men's lives? How did they think this was possible?
7. Explain the music of the spheres.
8. What are some of the relics in Greek notation that we have?

LISTENING ASSIGNMENT

2000 Years of Music or *VHMS*, Vol. I: Greek Music.

FOOTNOTES

¹This is the principal distinguishing feature between lyre and harp families. In the latter, the soundboard is always in a plane vertical to that of the strings. David's "harp" was really a lyre.

the golden age
of monophony

The Greeks brought intellect and science to music, but neither their intellect, their science, nor all their gods could save their society from becoming subject to Rome. The breath and soul of Western music was a heritage from people who had suffered under another, earlier bondage and had won freedom through courage and the mercy of their one God. To find the sources of Christian music and liturgy we turn to His Chosen People, the Jews.

In the year 516 B.C., seventy years after the destruction of the first building, the Jewish Temple was rebuilt. In the Temple, and there only, all sacrificial liturgy took place. But not all the people could come to the Temple, so in twenty-four outlying districts *Ma'amadot* were established. These were emissaries sent to the Temple two weeks out of every year to be present in person during the sacrifice, while in each district people assembled for prayer so they could attend at least in spirit. This spiritual service is said to be the origin of the synagogue. Hence, there were many synagogues but never more than one Temple.

The Temple liturgy was sacrificial; the burnt offering continued well into the first century A.D. It was conducted by priests and Levites, with nearly the total exclusion of the layman. The service was in a liturgical language which the people did not understand. Barred by language from understanding the mysteries, they came to the Temple mainly for the blessing of the priest after the sacrifice, although they did join in psalm singing and prayers.

The synagogue liturgy had more the characteristics of a spiritual service, based on elements of prayer, praise, devotion, and thanksgiving.

Readings from the scriptures were selected in accordance with the time of the liturgical year. These consisted of passages that would be for the edification of the people and were followed by an interpretation: a model for the lesson and sermon of the Christian service.

Prayers were offered in the synagogue three times daily, for each of which there were stereotyped formulas at the beginning and end, the middle sections being flexible and extemporized. At three places in the service, the *Qdusha*, from which came the *Sanctus* of the Christian church, was rendered responsorially. (GlE, p. 1.)

MUSIC IN HEBREW LITURGY

In responsorial singing, a group or congregation answers a leader. One marked trait of Hebrew poetry is the division of a verse into two parallel members. Thus, the leader or soloist might sing the first half of a verse and the congregation might answer with the second half, which often intensifies or contrasts with the first, as in Psalm 135:

Praise ye the Lord, praise ye the name of the Lord; praise
Him, O ye servants of the Lord.
Ye that stand in the house of the Lord, in the courts of
the house of our God.

Or, the second half might be a literal repetition every time, as in each of the twenty-six verses of Psalm 136:

O give thanks unto the Lord, for He is good; for His mercy
endureth forever.
O give thanks unto the God of Gods; for His mercy endureth
forever.

Psalms and prayers were sung in the synagogue and led by Levites in the Temple. Many passages in the Bible tell us about general participation by the people in singing and the playing of instruments before as well as after the time of David and Solomon; the first professional musicians in Hebrew history were among the Levites. These were men especially appointed by King David to provide music for Temple worship, which included the use of double-reed instruments, trumpets, cymbals, harps, and lyres, in addition to a chorus of men and boys.

Important features of the Christian service had precedent in Jewish customs as well as in the liturgy. The Passover, celebrated in the home from its earliest beginnings, is a complicated service taking place on the fourteenth of Nisan, or early April. Bitter herbs and unleavened bread have long served as a reminder of the privation experienced on the flight from Egypt. The son or youngest child would ask, "What do these things signify?" The father replied with the story of slavery and liberation.

Following this was the meal proper. The father took the unleavened bread, blessed it, and broke it, passing it around the family, thus symbolizing brotherly communion in one bread. Then all sang the first part

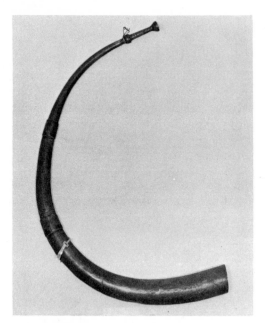

Figure 6. Roman **cornu**. Facsimile of an instrument in the British Museum. (Courtesy of Instrument Museum, Brussels.)

of the *Hallel* (beginning with Psalm 113), responding after each verse with "Hallelujah," which means "Praise to Jehovah."

After the meal, the father would raise the cup newly filled with wine and give thanks, whereupon all drank of it.

When the father of the Hebrew family passed the bread he would say, "See the bread of misery eaten by our fathers who passed out of Egypt."

THE MASS AND OFFICE

It was at a Passover meal that Christ said when He handed the bread to the disciples, "This is my body which is given for you."

The Eucharist or Communion of the Christian Church, the Mass, is a symbolic re-enactment of that Passover meal and a commemoration of Christ's sacrifice on the Cross. In the early Christian community, too, it first took place in connection with a meal. The first Christians, being Jews, continued to observe the liturgy of the Jewish law, in which everyone regularly took part. But there was in addition the new Christian aspect symbolizing the Last Supper. Until the end of the first century the first Christians, in addition to attending regular synagogue services, had special meetings in their homes with symbolic breaking of bread before the meal and the cup of blessing at the end. Thus, the first Mass was really a home Mass.

The early Eucharist was often preceded by an agape (ăg'-à-pē), a festival of brotherly love with prayers, songs, and an offering for the poor. From the agape may have come some of the earliest Mass formulas still preserved: "The Lord be with you. And with thy Spirit. Lift up your hearts. We have lifted them up to the Lord. Let us give thanks to the Lord our God. It is meet and right so to do." (Omn, p. 6.)

Soon after separating from the synagogues the Christians had meetings in their own private buildings. The meal in connection with the Eucharist was discontinued when the gatherings became too large for all the people to be seated at table.

Christians did not withdraw from Jewish worship until the end of the first century, so they appeared in synagogues in various places around the Mediterranean, converting large numbers of Jews and Greeks, many of whom had become Jews. Palestinian Jews and many Hellenists carried the Christian creed along the African coast and from there into Spain, southern Gaul, and southern Italy.

Growth and Development of the Liturgy

In the second century the Christian service became somewhat stabilized and the basic structure of the Mass began to emerge. It was divided into two main parts: the first, based on the word of the Scriptures, was for the new converts, the unbaptized, called *catechumens*, and consisted of readings from the Old and New Testaments, prayers, psalm singing, and a sermon for the instruction of the new converts, after which they were dismissed. This "sending away," or *missio*, developed into a name for the Mass as a whole: the source of the word *Missa*, the Latin name for the Mass, is in the final words of the liturgy, *Ite, missa est.*

The second part of the Mass liturgy, for the faithful, the baptized, was the Eucharist itself. The first section, for the catechumens, was strongly influenced by the synagogue service; the second had more the character of a sacrifice, as in the Temple.

Prayers opened and closed with stereotyped formulas, the central sections having been improvised. The oldest procedure in psalm singing was responsorial in which the soloistic passages were usually performed by a trained singer. Philo of Alexandria, who lived in the first century, relates instances of antiphonal singing as well. This occurs when two choruses or half choruses sing in alternation.

conversion of constantine

Although the main outlines of the Mass took general shape in the third century, there was still no fixed wording for the liturgy. The fourth century was one of tremendous significance in the growth of the Christian church and its music. The spark from which the blaze grew was a proclamation, one of the greatest events in history. Eusebius in his *Life of Constantine* relates that one noonday the emperor saw a flaming cross in the sky with the Greek words for "By this conquer," a factor leading to the emperor's conversion to Christianity. It was the Edict of Milan, arising out of a conference between Constantine and Licinius in 313, that assured toleration for the Christian church after its long trial of suffering.

With the removal of all fear of persecution the church enjoyed enormous growth from the fourth century on. Important centers at first were Alexandria and Antioch and, soon thereafter, Byzantium, destined to become the hub of the Greek Catholic church. It was in the near east that celebration of the mysteries began to take on great splendor, with beautiful vestments, lights, incense, and solemn processions. The liturgical language at first was Greek — even in Rome for several centuries this was standard.

music in the early christian services

While the liturgy was taking shape musical expression grew out of and along with the liturgical forms. Singing was a part of the earliest Christian customs — *Hallel* was sung at the Last Supper. Singing and making melody in your heart to the Lord is mentioned in Paul's Epistles to the Ephesians 5:19 and to the Colossians 3:16. Singing in the heart is prayer. Chant, or plainsong, is not just an ornament but a fundamental part of the liturgy. In this sense singing has always been worship itself, an integral part of the word; in this sense it was born of the word, inseparable from it. Often the extremely close connection between a text and its melody, showing how naturally they belong together, may be easily seen in pieces of chant included in modern collections. In many instances the highest notes of the musical setting of a word are so placed that they correspond with the syllable that is accented when the word is spoken, as in Figure 7.

Instrumental music did not fare well in the early years of the church, largely because it was associated with pagan customs. Early officials of the church considered it wiser to stay away from all practices that might remind new converts of heathen associations. Instruments produced music for enjoyment, which was not the purpose of liturgical music — music of the spirit, music of worship.

At first, women as well as men took part in singing. However, church officials overzealously interpreted passages in the Epistles: "Let your women keep silence in the churches," and "Let the woman learn in silence," so that eventually singing by women in the church was banned. By the fourth century choirs consisted of men and boys.

growth of roman chant

With new Christian communities springing up everywhere it became necessary for the text of the liturgy to be standardized and approved for general use. Widely separated areas around the Mediterranean developed their own liturgical texts and melodies. Distinct liturgies and their music were the Roman, Milanese, Coptic in North Africa, Mozarabic in Spain, Gallican in Gaul, and Celtic in the British Isles. Eventually Roman chant replaced nearly all of these; Pepin the Short decreed the substitution of Roman for Gallican liturgy in 754. His son Charle-

Figure 7. Beginning of **Jubilate Deo,** Offertory for the Second Sunday after Epiphany. (From MV, published by Desclée & Cie, Tournai, Belgium, 1957. Photo used by special permission.)

magne, who could read but never learned to write, brought singers from Rome to improve and standardize the services of the church. Mozarabic chant was finally replaced by Roman in the eleventh century. Milanese chant was the only other Western chant to survive and is still sung in that city. (HAM, No. 10; ParT, Nos. 1, 2, and 3.)

There was soon a tremendous demand for singers to go forth and carry Roman chant to parishes away from Rome. These singers received training at the *Schola Cantorum,* supposed to have been organized by Pope Sylvester in the fourth century. Originally the Roman papal choir, singers remained there long enough to learn the rapidly growing repertory of Roman chant. Since there was as yet no means of written notation, these hundreds of melodies could be learned only by hearing them sung. Comparisons made between forms aurally transmitted over many centuries in widely separated localities reveal astonishing resemblances.

Even more astounding are the results of research by the late Abraham Idelsohn of Hebrew Union College in Cincinnati. He discovered that melodies sung in scattered Jewish communities, isolated from each other since the first Temple was destroyed in 586 B.C., are not only counterparts of each other but also of some occurring in Roman chant. Ancient Greek music, too, may have contributed melodies to Roman chant — we know of at least one, for the notes of Seikilos' *Skolion* to his wife Euterpe (cf. p. 16) occur in order, although with other notes added and interpolated, in *Hosanna filio David,* part of the Roman liturgy for Palm Sunday. (ReMMA, p. 115.)

st. ambrose

Milanese liturgy and its chant are now called Ambrosian after St. Ambrose, the eloquent Bishop of Milan from 374 to his death in 397. He successfully resisted efforts of the young pagan Emperor Valentinian II and the Empress Justina to weaken the position of Christianity in northern Italy. In his campaign against Justina and the heretics he seized on a literary and musical form that Hilary of Poitiers had brought back from the eastern Mediterranean: the hymn.

A spontaneous, poetic song in praise of God, the hymn had its place in Christian worship in the time of Christ and the apostles. Many of the earliest ones before 300 were destroyed because their texts were not from the Bible. In the fourth century, however, there was a new growth of hymn writing. First widely cultivated in Syria, hymns have been useful many times as vehicles for conveying new Christian doctrines.

St. Ambrose was very successful in using hymns in his struggle against the Empress Justina. How many he wrote we do not know —

only four are authoritatively ascribed to him: *Deus Creator omnium,*
Iam surgit hora tertia, Aeterne rerum conditor, and the Christmas hymn
Veni, Redemptor gentium. Written in dignified simplicity, their form has
been the model for many later ones. Their standard structure consists of
eight four-line stanzas in iambic tetrameter. Nearly all hymns have been
written in some metrical pattern, an important exception being the
Te Deum. (HAM, No. 9; GlE, p. 2.)

To St. Ambrose may also belong the credit for having introduced antiphonal singing into Western chant. Records show he trained his adher-
ents in this technique at the time of the persecution by Empress Justina.

pope gregory I

During the course of the fourth century old chants became stabilized
and many new ones were added. Much of the development may have
been due to the *Schola Cantorum,* which grew and thrived under the
interest and encouragement of several popes: Celestine I, Sixtus III, and
especially Leo the Great.

The pope who is traditionally credited with the most significant and
extensive contributions to the history of Roman plainsong is Gregory I.
As a result, the music of the Roman liturgy is now usually called
Gregorian chant. However, the importance of his role has diminished
as research reveals that much of what he was supposed to have done
can be traced to earlier times. His main accomplishment now seems to
have been a reorganization of existing melodies; also, he may have been
the one who did the most to assign to certain chants their places in the
liturgical year. Even the book he was once thought to have assembled,
the *Antiphonal* or *Antiphonary,* may have been in existence by his time.

Collections of Liturgical Music

The modern *Antiphonal* has in it the texts and music of the antiphons of the *Breviary,* the book containing daily prayers for the *Office*
or *Canonical Hours.* An antiphon is a short text with its own melody,
used principally to precede and follow the chanting of a psalm or can-
ticle. The Office is the liturgy for the daily private worship of priests
and others who devote their lives to the service of the Catholic church.
The services of the Office occur eight times every day of the year. They
are called, in order, *Matins* (before dawn), *Lauds* (at dawn), *Prime*
(6 A.M.), *Terce* (9 A.M.), *Sext* (noon), *None* (3 P.M.), *Vespers* (before nightfall), and *Compline* (after nightfall).

Certain texts and their melodies from the Office have figured prominently in later music history, especially the *Magnificat,* the Virgin's

hymn of praise after the Annunciation (part of Sunday Vespers), and certain antiphons dedicated to the Virgin (part of Sunday Compline): *Alma Redemptoris Mater, Ave Regina caelorum, Regina caeli,* and *Salve Regina.*

Many parts of text and music for the Office are also in the modern collection called *Liber Usualis* of which the principal portion, however, consists of text and music for the Mass. Thus, the Liber is the most comprehensive collection of Roman chant. The *Gradual* duplicates much of the Liber; it has the texts and music of the Mass sung by the choir, also found in the *Missal*, which contains all that is said or sung at Mass.

Organization of Plainsong

Musical portions of the Mass are in two classifications, the *Ordinary* and the *Proper*. The former consists of five sections whose texts never change, although different melodies for each of these are available in the Liber and the Gradual. There are eighteen settings for the Ordinary printed in modern chant books. These provide a variety of melodies for the *Kyrie, Gloria, Sanctus,* and *Agnus* and four principal settings for the *Credo*. Following these are a number of ad libitum melodies for each.

The Proper contains other texts and their melodies for use according to the time of the liturgical year or for special occasions, such as the Mass for Easter Sunday and the Mass for the Dead (*Requiem*); for individual saints' days (Mass for St. Andrew the Apostle), or special festivals (Mass for the Dedication of a Church). Thus, in most cases the various portions of the Proper are heard only once a year. Following is the order of the Ordinary and Proper:[1]

Ordinary	Proper
	Introit
Kyrie	
Gloria	
	Gradual
	Alleluia or Tract
Credo	
	Offertory
Sanctus and Benedictus	
Agnus Dei	
	Communion

music of the ordinary and proper

Introit ("He comes in"). In the older cathedrals the clergy usually prepared for the service in a room not far from the entrance, well removed from the altar. The Introit and Communion are antiphonal; all other chants of the Proper (with one exception, see below) are responsorial.

After the Introit, all antiphons and the chanting of psalms, comes the *Gloria Patri*, also called the Lesser Doxology. In chant books its performance is indicated by the abbreviation *e u o u a e*, the letters being the vowels of the last two words of its Latin text, *Seculorum. Amen.* ("Forever and ever. Amen.")

The *Kyrie*. The form now used consists of three sections: Kyrie I, Christe, Kyrie II, each consisting, respectively, of a threefold repetition of the phrases *Kyrie eleison* ("God have mercy on us"), *Christe eleison* ("Christ have mercy on us"), *Kyrie eleison*. Formerly there were many more repetitions in a litany-like manner and the congregation used to take part, these changes having been made about the end of the ninth century. For thirteen of the eighteen Kyrie settings the music is in the form AAA BBB CCC'; these, the oldest and simpler than the rest, are probably the ones in which congregations once participated. The words are a remnant of the times when the liturgical language was Greek, which was replaced by Latin about the beginning of the fourth century. The Kyrie is therefore one of the oldest parts of the liturgy.

Gloria in excelsis Deo ("Glory be to God on high"). Originally a morning hymn based on the words of the Christmas angel, it is called the Greater Doxology. The first four words of the text are always intoned by the celebrant alone; thereafter, beginning with the words *Et in terra pax*, the choir joins in.

Gradual. The Epistle and Gospel are read from an elevated lectern called an *ambo*. On a step — *gradus* — leading up to this lectern the priest sang the soloistic part of the Gradual.

Alleluia. This part of the Proper, being an expression of intense religious joy and happiness, is one of the most florid and elaborate in Mass or Office. Taken directly from Jewish rites, it is extremely old. The last syllable of the word receives especially ornate treatment, being set to a long, extended passage called the *jubilus*.

Tract. In seasons of repentance and mourning, such as during Lent and in the Mass for the Dead, the Tract takes the place of the joyous Alleluia. Among the Tracts are some of the oldest surviving chant melodies. This is the one chant in the Mass that is neither responsorial nor antiphonal; it is in *direct* psalmody, originally for a soloist with no choral answer.

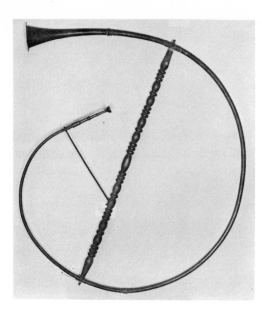

Figure 8. Roman **tuba curva.** Facsimile of an instrument found in the ruins of Pompeii. (Courtesy of Instrument Museum, Brussels.)

Credo. The first ecumenical council in the history of the Christian church took place at Nicaea in 325. The delegates formulated the first version of the Nicene Creed which since then has been expanded, the present text having been agreed on at the Council of Chalcedon in 451. Genuflexion during *Et incarnatus est* was a custom introduced in the eleventh centrury. As in the case of the Gloria, the celebrant alone intones the opening phrase, *Credo in unum Deum* ("I believe in one God"), the choir joining in at *Patrem omnipotentem* ("Father almighty").

Offertory. Here begins the liturgy of the sacrifice. At this point in the service priests, singers, and members of the congregation used to bring their gifts to the altar.

Sanctus. Its threefold intonation ("Holy, Holy, Holy") is patterned after that of the *Qdusha.* At first the Sanctus was sung by the priest; then the congregation joined in. Thus, the earliest of these settings, too, are quite simple, later ones being more elaborate. The use of the bell originated about the thirteenth century.

Agnus Dei ("Lamb of God"). For the reason already given these melodies, too, were simpler at first. Usually the melodies of the Ordinary bear little or no resemblance to each other; however, the Sanctus and Agnus of Mass XVII form an exception.

Communion. Chants of the Communion bear some stylistic resemblance to those of the Introit.

Although Mass may be celebrated any time of any day, it is usually during the morning because on whatever day it is said the priest must fast until after Mass takes place. For High Mass the complete ceremony with full musical participation by choir and priest is necessary; for Low Mass the priest alone may recite all the texts in a quiet voice.

Plainsong is monophonic, impersonal, objective, and impassionate. It is an ideal medium for expressing the sacred texts of the liturgy — the music is part of the liturgical act itself.

the modes

Analysis of the arrangement of half and whole steps in chant melodies reveals that there are eight ways in which they are ordered within an octave. We refer to these eight octave species as the *ecclesiastical, church,* or *medieval modes.* In each of these modes one note, called the *finalis,* is the one on which melodies in that mode usually end. In each mode a different note, called the *tenor, tuba,* or *reciting tone,* is favored as the one on and around which the greater part of the singing is done. If we place the notes used in any one of these eight modes within an octave in accordance with the range of the melodies in that mode, we find the internal arrangement can be conveniently compared to one of eight combinations of white keys on the piano:

		Range[2]	*Finalis*	Reciting tone	
1.	Dorian	d-d'	d	a	(5)
2.	Hypodorian	A-a	d	f	(6)
3.	Phrygian	e-e'	e	c'	(6)
4.	Hypophrygian	B-b	e	a	(7)
5.	Lydian	f-f'	f	c'	(5)
6.	Hypolydian	c-c'	f	a	(6)
7.	Mixolydian	g-g'	g	d'	(5)
8.	Hypomixolydian	d-d'	g	c'	(7)

The names of the modes were borrowed from terms the Greeks applied to octave species; musically the Greek modes were not the same as the medieval ones.

It may be seen in the above list that the modes group themselves in pairs: Dorian and Hypodorian, Phrygian and Hypophrygian, and so forth. Each pair has the same *finalis,* though within each pair there is a difference in the position of the reciting tone and in the relation of range

and *finalis*. The modes having the *finalis* as the first note in each range
(Nos. 1, 3, 5, and 7) are called the authentic modes; those having the
finalis as the fourth note in each range are called the plagal modes
(Nos. 2, 4, 6, and 8). Some melodies that we sing today are authentic
in the above sense — such as "Joy to the World," the entire melody of
which lies in the octave between two tonic notes (corresponding roughly
with the *finalis* in chant). Others are plagal, such as "O Come, All Ye
Faithful," because the melody lies in the octave between two dominant
notes (corresponding roughly with the reciting tone), with the tonic as
the fourth note in the range. The latter tune was taken from "Adeste
fideles," a plainsong melody in the sixth mode (plagal), on page 1870
of the Liber.[3] The modes are often identified by their numbers as given
in the list: Mode 1 is Dorian, Mode 2 Hypodorian, and so forth.

In Roman chant only one degree inflection was permitted: a B could
be lowered to B♭ in certain circumstances, for example, if a melody
approached that note degreewise from below, then turned and descended as at the beginning of *Jubilate Deo* (see p. 23).

structure and style

Chant melodies, unlike those to which we are accustomed, do not
consist of successions of single notes. Basic units are little groups of
notes or melodic formulas of varying lengths. Melodies are constructed
or pieced together by arranging these units in a desired order. This is
also a heritage from the music of the Near East. Usually any given
formula belongs in one mode only, for example, the first six notes of
Jubilate Deo form a group associated with the first mode, while this
formula 𝄢 ♩♩♩♩♩♩ is characteristic of the fifth.

Plainsong may be classified in several styles. *Liturgical recitative*
is used for prayers and readings from the Scriptures. There are many
more text syllables than musical pitches (Example 2a). Notice the little
melodic formulas at the beginning, middle, and end, very typical of
liturgical recitative. (AM-T, p. 188 ff.) In the *syllabic style* the number
of individual pitches and the number of syllables are just about the
same (Example 2b). In the *neumatic style* a single syllable is sung to
one of the formulas of a few notes, referred to above. Most of that
portion of *Jubilate Deo* reproduced on page 23 is neumatic except the
setting of the syllable -*la*- in the second occurrence of *jubilate*. This
passage is a *melisma* exemplifying the *melismatic style* in which the number of musical pitches far exceeds the number of syllables so it is very
florid and ornate. The musical setting for the -*a of* the *ea* in Example 2c
is also a melisma. The Alleluia, especially its *jubilus*, is very melismatic.
(P & O, No. 2.)

Example 2.   Styles of chant.

LU, p. 764.

a.

Nunc di - mit - tis   ser - vum   tu - um   Do - mi - ne,

se - cun - dum   ver - bum   tu - um   in   pa   -   ce.

LU, p. 780.

b.

Vic - ti - mae   pa - scha - li   lau - des

LU, p. 779.

c.

in - e   a

Psalm Tones

Under the heading of liturgical recitative are the psalm tones, responsorial settings for entire psalms. Each of these, like Example 2a, is
divided into two sections, one for each half of the psalm verse, with
opening, middle, and closing formulas. The whole form includes an
antiphon and the Gloria Patri as follows:

1. Antiphon, with its plainsong melody.
2. Psalm, each verse set to the same psalm tone.
3. Gloria Patri set to the same psalm tone.
4. Antiphon repeated.

There are nine psalm tones, one for each of the church modes plus an
irregular one with two reciting tones. (P & O, No. 1.)

32

MUSIC THEORY OF THE MIDDLE AGES

A number of treatises written by scholars of the Middle Ages are important for two reasons. In the first place, this literature preserves information about the music of antiquity; second, by means of these manuscripts this knowledge was transmitted to and used by other writers of the Middle Ages and later. Some of these treatises were intended for the instruction of beginners while others dealt with more advanced ideas in theory.

Boethius (c.480-524), Cassiodorus (c.485-c.580), and Isidore of Seville (c.570-636) were the authors whose treatises preserved much of the information we have about Greek music. Some of the later writers duplicated material written by these three.

The *Dialogus* which may have been by Odo of Cluny (d. 942) is the oldest existing source associating letter names with pitches in a manner thereafter to become standard. The work is one of many didactic conversations between pupil and master, who in this case instructs his student in the musical gamult of the Greeks from A to a' as adapted for use in the Middle Ages by adding G below and b', c", d", and e" above.

Music Notation

We know that attempts to write music were made by the middle of the eighth century, but no examples come down to us before those of the

Figure 9. Neumes of the ninth century from a manuscript in St. Gall, Switzerland. (From PalMC, published by Desclée & Cie, Tournai, Belgium, 1924.)

ninth. The earliest signs used for writing music are called neumes. They are believed to have had their origin in grammatical signs of Greek and Latin, indicating that the voice was to be raised (/) or lowered (\ ). These neumes were a kind of shorthand system, the symbols of which, without any staff lines or any other method of showing exact pitches, were written above the texts that were chanted. Thus, because of the attendant inexactness, all these signs showed was whether the melody went up or down, with perhaps some indications of rhythm. The principal value of the neumes was to serve as a prop to the memory of a singer who at some previous time had learned the melodies in the chant repertory.

There was an improvement when the neumes became heighted — that is, the scribes of the manuscripts attempted to show by placing the neumes in proper height relationships how many scale degrees any

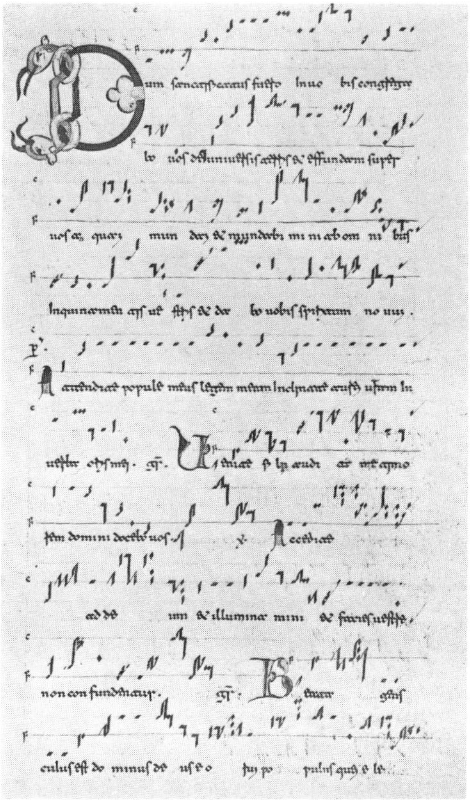

Figure 10. Rudimentary staff notation of the eleventh century from a manuscript in Benevento. (From PalMG, published by Desclée & Cie, Tournai, Belgium, 1937.)

given note was to be sung above or below the one preceding. Heighted neumes were written in straight, horizontal rows but with no lines drawn. The next step was to draw lines indicating definite pitches: first, about the beginning of the eleventh century, was a red line with the letter F to indicate the f below middle c′; second, was a yellow one with the letter C to indicate middle c′; third, was a green one with a G for our middle g′. Modern clefs developed from these capital letters. Guido of Arezzo (d. 1050) is believed to have been the one who perfected the staff system already begun. For many centuries clef signs were moved at will so leger lines would not be needed. The F and C clefs were the most common throughout the Middle Ages and the Renaissance, G clefs making more frequent appearances in the Baroque:

Example 3.   The clefs, old and modern, show how middle C would be notated in each.

Modern chant notation still depends on movable C and F clefs. A sign called the *custos* ("guardian") placed at the end of each set of staff lines shows what the first note on the next staff will be. In modern plain-song, vertical lines indicate the ends of small melodic divisions, members of a phrase, phrases, or the end of a piece of chant.[4]

Solmization and Hexachords

Guido may also have been the one to perfect a system of sight sing-ing. The notes of the medieval gamut were arranged in groups of six called hexachords. In each hexachord the sequence of tones and semi-tones was TTSTT. A hexachord might begin on G, c, f, g, c', f', or g'. A name was given to each kind of hexachord: it was called *durum* ("hard") if it contained B-natural (beginning on a G), *molle* ("soft") if it contained B-flat (beginning on an F), and *naturale* if neither was present (beginning on a C). There is a Gregorian hymn to St. John, each half line of which begins a scale degree higher than the one before, the first starting on c. Thus, each half line begins on the successive notes of the natural hexachord:

Figure 11. Beginning of Hymn to St. John, **Ut queant laxis.** (From LU, published by Desclée & Cie, Tournai, Belgium, 1947. Photo used by special permission.)

The text syllables belonging with each of these six notes (*ut, re, mi, fa, sol, la*) were selected to be used as movable solmization syllables for each of the three hexachords in any octave in which the hexachords might appear (Example 4). When a seventh syllable was needed it was provided by the initials of the last two words of that hymn stanza, *Sancti Ioannes: si.*

To aid singers in learning solmization a mnemonic device called the Guidonian hand (although Guido may not have invented it) is offered in certain old manuscripts. Various phalanges of the left hand each represent one degree of the medieval gamut. In training his choir the director could point to any of these phalanges to indicate the note he wanted them to sing.

NORTHWARD SPREAD OF PLAINSONG

During the lifetime of Gregory I the music he reorganized and codified began its journey to the north. Augustine of Kent (d. c.613), who became the first Bishop of Canterbury, carried Gregorian chant to England in 598. Irish monks and some Scottish ones who emigrated to the continent in the eighth century added strength to Pepin's move to discard Gallican in favor of Roman chant.

Example 4.   Notes in the medieval hexachord system.

Hard hexachords are in italics; soft hexachords,
boldface; natural hexachords, ordinary type.

The impress of the northern personality brought some changes and
important additions. The motion of chant melodies at the time they
were carried from Rome to peripheral areas is believed to have been
predominantly stepwise. Music of the east, on which chant was originally
based, is essentially diatonic; when skips occur, the fourth is the interval usually favored. Curt Sachs has shown that indigenous music of
northern Europe, on the other hand, strongly favors melodic motion in
thirds. Northerners who became priests and members of sacred orders

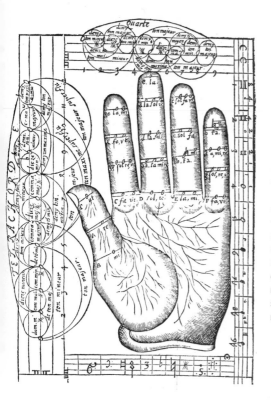

Figure 12. The hand and its musical significance. The Guidonian hand was an ingenious aid to sight-singing. Guido divided the scale into six intervals, or the hexachord: **ut, re, mi, fa, sol, la.** The leader of a choir pointed to the corresponding phalanges of his own fingers to show choir members which syllables to sing. (Courtesy of The Bettman Archive.)

were born with this music in their ears, so it is not surprising that intervals of a third and intervals formed by combinations of thirds (a fifth = two thirds), or even chains of thirds, began to affect plainsong as old chant melodies were performed north of the Alps and as new ones were added. Certain northern monasteries became especially important centers in chant composition, such as those at Reichenau in southern Germany and St. Gall in Switzerland. New additions and alterations enriched the chant repertory for many hundred years after the death of Gregory I. So many changes were made in the original plainsong after its introduction into northwestern Europe that one should distinguish between Gregorian chant and Medieval chant.

Tropes and Sequences

Interest and concentration in the history of music is being continually shifted to eras farther and farther back in the distant past. Medieval music is now attracting the attention of increasing numbers of the best

young scholars. As a result, some theories once considered correct must
be reconsidered. One of the most important of these is the long-estab-
lished, but now questioned theory concerning tropes and sequences. For
a long time the idea was that a trope was an interpolation, sometimes
of text, sometimes of music, or both, into official, pre-existent liturgical
chant. But the chant was in such a process of development and change
in the second half of the Middle Ages that it would be impossible to
define precisely what was "official." Also, most of the melodies of Ordinaries now in chant books are Medieval, not Gregorian. It may well be
that the trope, both music and text, were all part of the original composition.

In the case of the Kyrie trope, for example, it is now suggested that
the musical setting was composed originally for the combined text of
Example 5b and that Example 5a now in the chant books was the result
of omitting the extra words between *Kyrie* and *eleison* and was therefore the more recent, not the older version. Similar conditions may hold

Example 5.   Kyrie IV and Omnipotens genitor trope.

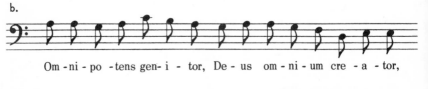

true for other troped plainsong settings. At the Council of Trent (1545-1563) all tropes were banned from the repertory. (See also Omn, p. 12f.)

The sequence has been regarded as a special kind of trope applied to the long, intricate musical settings of the *jubilus*, the last syllable of the Alleluia. The form of the Alleluia is ABA': Alleluia — Psalm verse — Alleluia plus expansion or elaboration. It is now thought that originally the sequence may have been a section of text and melody either to be substituted for the repetition of the Alleluia or to be interpolated as an expansion of the second Alleluia.

The sequence eventually became very elaborate, with long, strophic poetic texts and musical settings. Two famous ones are *Victimae paschali laudes*, part of the Easter Sunday Mass and *Dies irae*, belonging to the Mass for the Dead. All but five sequences including the above two were also banned by the Council of Trent. (HAM, No. 16; Omn, pp. 4 and 10; P & O, No. 3; GIE, p. 4.)

Liturgical Drama

The earliest liturgical dramas date from about the tenth century. They were insertions into the liturgy, in dramatic dialogue, for presentation at Christmas or Easter. One of the first-known examples occurred in the Easter Mass and consisted of a short conversation, beginning: *Quem quaeritis* ("Whom seek ye?") between the angel and the two Marys who went to the tomb on Easter morning. Sacred dramas of the eleventh century and later were full-length entertainments staged with action and music. They dealt with biblical stories, such as *The Play of Daniel, The Play of Herod, The Wise and the Foolish Virgins*, and *The Maastricht Easter Play*. (ParT, No. 5; VHMS, Vol. II.)

SECULAR MONODY

Very few facts about secular music in the first ten centuries have come down to us. Few people outside the church knew how to write and those within the church were not interested in preserving secular repertory. As we know, it was not possible to notate any music until about the eighth century. We have only isolated bits of information concerning the beginnings.

The first secular poet of the Middle Ages of whom we have knowledge was Venantius Fortunatus, Bishop of Poitiers (530-609), who also wrote the hymns, *Vexilla Regis proderunt* ("The Royal Banners Forward Go") and *Pange lingua gloriosi lauream* ("Sing, my tongue, the glorious battle"). Some Latin lyrics, among them a song of spring, were written in Rome in the sixth century. Irish monks who wandered to the continent wrote lyrics on secular subjects. There were some heroic songs of the Carolingian era. An eleventh-century collection is called the *Cambridge Songs*. The *Carmina Burana* — love songs, drinking songs, with some satire — are preserved with their melodies in a thirteenth-century manuscript, but these are written in staffless neumes. Texts of all the earliest secular songs were in Latin.

For many years students and members of the clergy traveled about singing their Latin songs. Wanderers of the eleventh and twelfth centuries are called goliards. (Omn, p. 13; GlE, p. 7.) Itinerant performers who sang in the vernacular were called *jongleurs*. They sang heroic lyrics and *chansons de geste*, epic narrations also on heroic subjects (*Chanson de Roland*). They were people of very low rank, mainly tricksters with a variety of facile kinds of entertainment.

Troubadours and Trouvères

The first-known secular poetry in the vernacular also appeared near Poitiers, in the territory of the Duke of Acquitaine. Guillaume IX (c.1071-1127) is said to have been the first of the Provençal group we call the troubadours. In two important respects the jongleurs differed from the troubadours and their counterpart in northern France, the trouvères: members of the last two groups were noblemen, and they were authors and composers rather than performers. Their works were performed by a jongleur, who might receive a permanent appointment as minstrel to the court. Troubadours and trouvères could afford to have their poetry and music copied in beautifully illuminated song collections called *chansonniers*. Very rarely might a person of low rank become a troubadour if he could write the texts and their melodies and find favor at court. Such a one was Bernard de Ventadorn, who rose from a scullery. Other famous troubadours were Marcabru and Geoffre Rudel. The troubadours flourished in the twelfth century.

The granddaughter of Guillaume IX, Eleanor of Acquitaine, married a northerner who became King of France. She took with her Bernard de Ventadorn, and it was perhaps her influence that helped stimulate the trouvères, who were active from the mid-twelfth through the thirteenth centuries. Prominent among this group were Gace Brulé; Blondel de Nesle, minstrel to Richard the Lion-Hearted; Thibaut IV, King of Navarre; and Adam de la Halle, who wrote a little musical play called *Le Jeu de Robin et Marion* about the time when the Robin Hood legends were arising. (GlE, p. 16ff.)

The love songs of the troubadours and trouvères idealized their object of affection as though she were on a pedestal worshipped from afar. In addition the repertory contained poetic debates, discussions, crusaders' songs, spinning songs, laments, and dawn songs.

There was a wide variety of forms in which the songs of these two groups were written, but eventually there emerged three which we shall mention here because their popularity continued, forming the basic structures of many secular songs until past the end of the fifteenth century. Originally, these were songs people sang as they danced: those portions designated by a lower-case letter were sung by a leader; the other parts, shown in capital letters are refrain material sung by the whole group:

Rondeau: ABaAabAB   (Each letter refers to a single line.)
Virelai: AbbaA   } (Here the letters refer to sections, each of
Ballade: aab(C) }   which may consist of one or more lines.)

Refrains came at the beginning as well as the end of the first two; the refrain was not always present in the ballade. These three are known as the *formes fixes*. (HAM, Nos. 18 and 19; Omn, p. 13; P & O, No. 4; ParT, No. 6; GlE, pp. 8-15; AM-G, many examples.)

Germany and Spain

Very much like the ballade was the bar form, *aab*. This was a favorite among the minnesingers who flourished in Germany in the twelfth and thirteenth centuries. Their songs continue types composed by troubadours and trouvères. Their most famous representative was Walther von der Vogelweide. (HAM, No. 20; Omn, p. 14; P & O, No. 5; GlE, p. 20f; AM-G, p. 45ff.)

Spain's principal contribution to medieval monody was the collection *Las Cantigas de Santa María* made by Alfonso el Sabio (c.1226-1284), King of Castile and León, which includes nearly four hundred sacred as well as secular pieces. (ParT, No. 7.)

Dances and Instruments

In the thirteenth century dancing began a separate existence, independent of singing. Dance music was furnished by jongleurs, who played for many court occasions. One favorite dance was the *estampie*. Its form was organized in successions of lines, each often repeated with first and second endings: AA' BB' CC', and so forth. The form of the *ductia* was similar, but shorter. (HAM, Nos. 40 and 41; Omn, p. 14f; GlE, p.

13.) Directions accompanying some textless pieces tell us they were to be performed, for example, by a vielle player: *In seculum viellatoris.* (HAM, No. 32e; GlE, p. 58f.)

The *vielle* or *fidel* was a bowed string instrument usually with three, four, or five strings, sometimes including a drone plucked with the left thumb. Pegs, mounted in a peg disc (often heart-shaped), were at right angles to the belly of the instrument, which was either guitar- or pear-shaped. Rhythm and melody for the dance were also often provided by pipe and tabor which were played by one person, the three-holed pipe held and fingered by the right hand and the tabor, hanging by a string from the right little finger, struck by a stick held in the left hand.

PARALLEL ORGANUM

Hermann von Helmholtz, a nineteenth-century pioneer in the acoustics of music, once performed experiments in the psychology of music

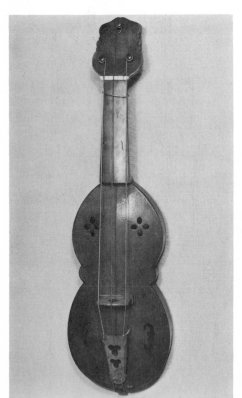

Figure 13. Vielle, reproduction of a sculpture on the portal of the Cathedral of Amiens. (Courtesy of the Instrument Museum, Brussels.)

that led to what is called the theory of fusibility. He found that there are people who experience difficulty in distinguishing between an octave, a perfect fifth, and a perfect fourth. Helmholtz theorized that people having these difficulties might easily believe they were singing correct pitches when actually they might be singing a perfect fifth or fourth away from the tones being sung by the rest of a group. Of course, men and women, or men and boys, sing in octaves and are aware of this. But when the group includes members having hearing defects like those just described, the result might be a performance in octaves, fifths, and fourths in parallel motion.

This is part-music in its simplest form. It is heard all over the world even in the present time among primitive tribes in Negro Africa, the Caucasus, and Central Asia. It still occurs in the singing of folk music in Iceland. It was written in manuscripts as late as the seventeenth century. It was observed in 1908 in the singing of an untrained congregation in France. It occurred during singing at the Civil Rights Rally in Jackson, Mississippi on June 26, 1966.

We do not know when this kind of singing began; however, in consideration of the wide range of its occurrence it is at least logical to believe it has been a continuous phenomenon extending farther back into the past than written history indicates. Music of this type is the product of a spontaneous attempt within a group to sing one and the same melody, but it sounds at different pitch levels resulting in two or more lines, or polylinear music.[5] It is always a phenomenon of group or choral singing.

Records of polylinear music date from the eighth century. The first clear description, however, is furnished by the unknown author of the Latin treatise *Musica Enchiriadis*, probably dated before 867. The term *órganum* (accent on the *first* syllable, pl. *órgana*), applied to this style of singing, antedated the work. Because the term later had other applications also, one should always say "parallel organum" when referring to the music now being discussed.

Information in the *Musica Enchiriadis* and elsewhere shows that in the ninth century parallel organum was not just spontaneous but a cultivated style. The basis for this polylinear music was a piece of chant selected from the plainsong repertory called the *vox principalis,* or "main voice." In parallel organum a second voice, duplicating the first melody and called the *vox organalis*, was added a fifth below the *vox principalis*. The *vox principalis* could be doubled an octave lower and the *vox organalis* an octave higher; the result would be quadrilinear music, a quadruple performance of the same melody.

Bilinear parallel organum may occur at the fifth or the fourth. In the course of this might occur the harmonic interval of an augmented fourth, also called the tritone (three whole steps), a dissonance to medieval ears. To avoid this, two voices would begin on a unison, the *vox organalis* remaining on the same note while the *vox principalis* moved degreewise upward until the interval of a fourth was reached. Thereafter both voices moved in parallel fourths until a few notes before the end of the phrase, when the two voices would move together again to end on a unison. (HAM, No. 25a and b; Omn, p. 15; P & O, No. 6; GlE, pp. 24-27; ML, V-1.)

In medieval treatises discussing parallel organum, it is primarily the choral portions of chant that are cited as examples to be used as the *vox principalis* in this polylinear style. Even in this cultivated form as well as in its spontaneous occurrence among untrained people, parallel singing has been generally choral, and to be associated with group performance. Because all voices of the music are the same or nearly the same melody, hence not polyphony, parallel organum is mainly an extension of monophonic music.

SOURCES AND ADDITIONAL READINGS

AuC	CrosM	KrüK	ReMMA
ApG	FeH	LU	SaH
BesA	GreD	MarD	SaRi
BessM	HelmS	MuC	StrS
BraI	IdJ	MV	UrC
ChT	JuM	PiH	WadS
CrT	KiP		WeS

LISTENING ASSIGNMENTS[6]

1. (a) *2000 Years of Music*: Jewish Music. What styles of chanting are represented? (b) *VHMS*, Vol. I: Jewish Music.
2. (a) *VHMS*, Vol. II: Mozarabic, Ambrosian, Gregorian chant; Liturgical Drama; Secular Monody; Parallel Organum. (b) ParT, Nos. 1-7: Ambrosian, Gallican, Mozarabic, Gregorian chant; Liturgical Drama; Secular Monody.
3. The Easter Mass. How would you describe the style of the music and manner of delivery; for example, is it intense, passionate, personal, subjective?
4. (a) P & O, No. 1. What difference do you notice in the singing of the halves of the psalm verses? Is this responsorial or antiphonal singing? Do you notice any printed sign at the point where the change takes place?

(b) P & O, No. 2. In what style is the Alleluia? (c) P & O, No. 3. In letters, outline the form of the sequence melody.

5. *The Play of Daniel* (GrD).
6. *Reis glorios* (HAM, No. 18c). What was the intended purpose of this song? (See p. 41 and comments that come with the record.)
7. *Estampie* and *ductia* (HAM, Nos. 40 and 41; P & O, No. 12). Observe the form in pairs of lines.
8. P & O, No. 6: Parallel Organum. Which line is the *vox principalis*?

WRITTEN ASSIGNMENTS

1. What differences do you notice between Roman and Ambrosian chant in HAM, No. 10? Any similarity?
2. In either *Liber Usualis* or Gradual, find chant settings for the five parts of the Ordinary; or, turn to Omn, pp. 1-9. In what style of chant are melodies for the Kyrie? For the Gloria and Credo? For the prayer (beginning *Dominus vobiscum*) on p. 3 in Omn, or for Psalm 110 on p. 252 in the Liber?
3. With music before you, what is the easiest way to determine the mode of a piece of plainsong? What is the mode of each chant in the Easter Mass?
4. Are C or F clefs used in the notation of the Easter Mass in Omn or the Liber? What kind of clef is used to notate No. 1 in P & O?
5. Show how the letter designation for sections (*AbbaA*) of No. 4 in P & O equates the designation according to musical lines (*AB cc ab AB*). Write out a pattern, in letters, according to lines of music in No. 5.

FOOTNOTES

[1]The musical portions of the Roman Mass for Easter Sunday are in Omn, beginning on page 1; they are also in GlE with some parts omitted. This Mass is recorded on ARC 3090.

[2]In this book middle C is represented as c'; the octaves below c', in order, as c, C, and CC; those in ascending order, as c'', c''', and c''''.

[3]Page numbers from one edition to another of the Liber may vary slightly.

[4]Many examples of early notation are reproduced in facsimile in AM-T.

[5]I use the term *polylinear* to refer to music written in two or more melodic lines, whether these consist of essentially the same or totally different melodies. Thus, polylinear includes all polyphonic music, or polyphony, but not vice versa. By dictionary definition, polyphony refers to "composition in simultaneous and harmonizing *but melodically independent and individual* parts or voices" (italics mine). Because this does not correctly apply to more-than-one-line music of which all lines are essentially the *same* melody, the need for the new term may be seen. One may also use the terms *bilinear, trilinear*, etc., in place of *two-part, three-part*, etc., where "part" is in danger of being confused with "section."

[6]Whenever the printed music is available, look at it as you listen.

the beginnings
of polyphony

The medieval era, or a part of it, has long been called the Dark Ages because of its intellectual stagnation. The term is very applicable to the life of its people, most of whom were born and died in an unbroken darkness of ignorance. It is likely that at least ninety percent of the entire population had no schooling whatsoever. In all classes, superstition was rife. Your gardener might have told you in all seriousness that peach trees would grow pomegranates if sprinkled with enough goat's milk.

The isolation of the medieval village is inconceivable: most inhabitants went from cradle to grave knowing no more people than could be put into a couple of modern transcontinental jets. The peasant's wood, wattle, or thatched one-room house sheltered his livestock and his family in a filth that would take long to describe. It is no wonder that in England as late as the fourteenth century you might have been fined twenty shillings for calling a man a *rusticus*.

Many peasants were too poor to buy straw for a bed. This is easily understood when one considers taxes and fees they had to pay manor lords: a direct tax according to size and yield of a farm; a fee for baking bread in the lord's oven, plus a percentage of loaves baked; a fee for grinding flour in the lord's mill; a fee for crushing grapes in his wine press; and a fee for arbitrating disputes. Feudalism was at its height in the tenth century, but two hundred years later when near its ebb these fees were still exacted. A peasant worked almost more for his master than himself.

Under the system of feudalism, land and vassals were the lord's greatest wealth. Even most of the nobility were not educated — many a lord had to fumble awkwardly over books. We have seen that Charlemagne himself could not write. The tall, wax candle by the lord's bedside was to keep pixies and the devil away; his main source of artificial light was a smoky, resinous torch. The lords themselves had masters and kings over them in an organization designed originally for protection against Norse, Moslem, or Magyar invaders. They had obligations as deputies of the king, who gave them titles — *comites* (counts) and *duces* (dukes) — with land as a benefice to support themselves and their vassals.

By 1300 the main structure of feudalism had weakened, due largely to increase in trade that had begun as far back as the ninth century. The lords born to the manor turned to commerce so they could afford more luxuries. They learned to preserve meat by salting or boiling it; a particular delicacy was stag roasted whole and served with a hot sauce spiced with pepper — which, as we shall see, became a great luxury. Merchants settled in places of importance, so there was growth outside and around castles. The intensification of trade and industry nurtured the development of towns and cities. The town itself acquired a wall and became a fortress or burg, its inhabitants *burgeuses* or *bourgeoisie*. The burger had need for the butcher, baker, cobbler, carpenter, and mason. Craftsmen soon organized into guilds to protect their own interests and maintain high standards. But in the middle of the fourteenth century the Black Death, which traveled along trade routes, killed from a third to three-fourths of the population.

In times of travail or triumph, the parish church was a center of comfort and security. Since nearly all students in medieval universities were clergy, almost all learning was concentrated in the church. Some were sincere and conscientious in their devotion. Even before the time of Pope Gregory I many Christians withdrew from the world to live in small communities under stringent rules. Those of St. Benedict in 529 influenced later sacred orders: members could own no property and could eat no meat; in strict confinement, they were occupied with manual labor. But as early as the fifth and sixth centuries other servants of the church became so involved in secular affairs that merely to be a priest was not enough for them. Eventually bishoprics and abbeys became involved in the feudal system: monks owned serfs and sometimes a large part of the national wealth. Often parishioners knew their churchman was a great landlord. In 1301 near Torquay, England, there was a complaint because a vicar stored corn in the church and used to his own benefit trees blown down in the churchyard. When a peasant died his heirs might have to pay as a mortuary to the clergy some live-stock, or a large cooking utensil, or even his bed. Some high members of the clergy were also warriors and even became nobles. They were wealthy in the only wealth of any significance — land. Even some Bene-dictines succumbed to worldly temptations; in 1098 Robert of Cham-pagne objected so strongly that he broke away from them and started the Cistercian order. Objections to these and other abuses in high places took curious expression in the texts for one of the new forms of poly-phonic music.

THE NATURE OF POLYPHONY

We have seen that parallel organum has had a continuous history from its first written records in the early Middle Ages, or before, into our present time. Artistic polyphony was something new. It originated when voices began to move in opposite directions — one voice moved up as the other moved down.

When we speak of polyphony we usually have in mind a piece of music in which two or more melodies, sounding together in contrapuntal style, move independently. Usually, they are different melodies; how-ever, if a composer, or two or more performers treat the same melodic line in such a way that the voices begin one after the other as in a canon or round ("Three Blind Mice"), the result of this, too, is polyphony. An element basic to our idea of polyphony is that the melodies move in contrary or oblique motion most of the time; in the midst of this treat-ment of the lines some parallel motion may occur, but its use must be very limited and carefully regulated or the term *polyphony* will no longer be correctly applicable. In the strictest sense, the concept of extended parallel motion is foreign to polyphony.

Good polyphonic writing requires skill and experience acquired by special training. Even for performance most polyphonic music must be studied — the singers are trained to perform the composition. Therefore, true polyphony cannot be spontaneous, except perhaps in the case of a round. It is an art.

Polyphony was apparently found to be beyond the skill of medieval choirs, for early artistic polyphony was associated with music performed by those singers who had special ability and training: the soloists of the choir. A melody from plainsong was selected as the basis for poly-phony also, but this was soon chosen from the soloistic portions of the chant. This pre-existent melody is called a *cantus firmus* (pl., *cantūs firmi*), or "fixed melody," because in principle at least it was not to be changed. The new line was written as a decoration for soloistic sections of plainsong in the liturgy of important festivals of the church year: Christmas, Easter, Pentecost, and Ascension. When the polyphonic passage ended and the performers arrived at the beginning of the next choral section of plainsong, the usual monophonic performance was resumed. Thus, the first artistic polyphony was for soloists; it remained soloistic until the fifteenth century.

Another difference between parallel organum and polyphony, or polyphonic organum, was that in the manuscript sources of the new style scribes wrote the counterpoint above the *cantus firmus*. If performed separately these new, added melodies sound very much like pieces of original chant. The first composers' attempts seem to have been aimed at duplicating plainsong to make a new melody of a style and value equal to that of the original. The horizontal aspect received prime consideration. Obviously, the beginners in the composition of artistic polyphony had no skill or experience in this technique so the vertical aspect suffers when their work is judged by our more cultivated sense of hearing. If the earliest composers of polyphony regarded the vertical aspect at all we must remember that to them the combination of different melodies was a completely new phenomenon for which their ears were not prepared either through training or heritage. Nowadays we are surrounded almost from birth by contemporary harmonic combinations — the sound of organized harmony is part of our heritage. Even when composers of polyphony first began regulating vertical combination of tones, they based their principles on ideas quite foreign to our rules of harmony — theirs was just the first step in a journey of a thousand years.

EARLY CENTERS AND STYLES

Although there is some evidence of polyphony in the century preceding, one of the earliest sources is from the eleventh century: the *Winchester Troper*. This is a collection of more than one hundred fifty additions to troped portions of Kyries, Glorias, Alleluias, and Tracts, in which contrary motion appears, though rarely. Although the collection includes melodies that are for local feasts and therefore probably by English composers, at least some of the music is believed to have originated across the English Channel.

France was indeed the region that nurtured the first important artistic polyphony. The center of main significance in the early twelfth century was the Benedictine Abbey of St. Martial in Limoges in southern France. Three important manuscripts, now in the Bibliothèque Nationale in Paris, preserve its repertory. In these collections are examples of *conductus* (pl., *conductūs*), originally a new monophonic melody with a text of rhymed, metrical Latin poetry added to the Introit and used during the entrance of the clergy. Later the *conductūs* were simply rhymed Latin poems, primarily religious but also on a variety of subjects with the tunes newly composed for them. Polyphonic *conductūs* at St. Martial were for use in the Mass or Office, with emphasis on the Christmas season.

St. Martial Polyphony

Two principal styles are distinguishable in St. Martial polyphony. In one, the plainsong *cantus firmus* loses its identity as a melody because the notes are extended into long values. Thus, the *cantus firmus* is not recognizable in performance — it assumes the function of a basis for the composition of a new melody written above it in motion comparable to that of chant. The name tenor was soon used in reference to any bottom part in a polyphonic piece. (Omn, p. 15; P & O, No. 8; GlE, pp. 30 and 33.)

In other style of polyphony written at St. Martial both voices — the *cantus firmus* from plainsong and the new melodic counterpoint above it — move almost simultaneously. It is from the Latin name for motion *punctus contra punctum* ("note against note") that the term counterpoint is derived. (HAM, No. 26, No. 27a; GlE, p. 32.)

This abbey was the first real center of polyphonic writing. Its achievements were significant not only in establishing polyphonic styles that influenced later works, but also because polyphony there became firmly a part of the liturgical service.

Santiago di Compostela

Another important religious center of the twelfth century is at Compostela in northern Spain, legendary burial place of the Apostle St. James, named after him Santiago di Compostela. A famous goal of pilgrimage in the late Middle Ages, it became, first a repository for music contributed by pilgrims visiting there; second, it became a center from which this music radiated as pilgrims returned home or went on to other places. The *Codex Calixtinus* (c.1140), a manuscript preserved there, includes a polyphonic piece which may be by a Parisian. It is the oldest known example of trilinear polyphony, *Congaudeant catholici*. The third voice, in a style unlike that of the other two, is considered to be a later addition to what was originally a piece *a 2*. (GlE, p. 34.)

The Parisian School

In the reign of Louis VII (1137-1180), first husband of Eleanor of Acquitaine, an era of prolific creativity in polyphony began in various churches in Paris. Soon after 1150 the old, original cathedral of Notre Dame was torn down; the foundation for the new, present building was laid in 1163. Famous personalities helped the city become a center of culture even before the university was founded. For example, Peter Abelard (1079-1142) had been a leading figure at the old Notre Dame and other schools, attracting international acclaim. John of Salisbury (d.1180), who later became secretary to Thomas à Becket, was in Paris somewhat later, about the time musical composition began to flourish there. From him we have remarks about contemporary Parisian polyphony — he mentions long, ascending and descending passages with clashing of voices.

He may have been referring to music by Leonin, or Leoninus, the first person we know by name as a composer of polyphony. This man was probably active at the old cathedral and perhaps in other churches while the new one was being built. He is stated to have been the composer of the *Magnus Liber Organi* . . . . , a cycle of polyphonic graduals, alleluias, and responsories for the entire liturgical year. The source for much information about the Parisian school is an unknown Englishman who in the late thirteenth century visited Paris and wrote details about the late twelfth and early thirteenth-century music he heard there. He is called Anonymous IV because his Latin treatise is the fourth anonymous one in a collection of medieval treatises. He mentions by

Figure 14. Beginning of three-voiced organum **Descendit,** from Wolfenbüttel 1099 (1206), of which the two upper voices are in the rhythmic modes. For a transcription into modern notation, see Example 6. (From facsimile of the manuscript. Courtesy of the Institute of Mediaeval Music.)

Example 6. Transcription of Figure 14.

Beginning with the second measure the two upper voices are in the first mode; in the last four and a half measures they are in the third mode.

name also a second composer, Perotin, or Perotinus, who lived in the generation following Leonin.

The Parisian repertory does not duplicate that of St. Martial. The connection between the two repertories is mainly one of stylistic technique, because the two styles mentioned above (the one with *cantus firmus* in extended note values and the more homogeneous one written mostly note against note) are those principally employed in the earliest Parisian polyphony. At first, the number of voices did not exceed two.

the rhythmic modes

Leonin is usually credited with the first systematic attempts to regulate rhythm, although beginnings may have been made at St. Martial. Until this time the notes of polyphonic voices could be correlated for performance by carefully aligning them vertically in the manuscripts to show which notes were intended to occur together as harmonic intervals. The new rhythmic system was based on the mystic number three, representative of the Trinity. Binary division of a pulse was considered inferior to ternary. Each of a rhythmically regulated series of pulses was divided into three parts in any of six different ways we call the rhythmic modes. These modes are ternary arrangements of familiar types of poetic feet. In modern notation the time signature $\frac{6}{8}$ is applied to each mode as follows:

Mode 1   ♩ ♪♩ ♪   (trochaic)   Mode 4   ♪♩ ♩.   (anapaestic)

Mode 2   ♪♩ ♪♩   (iambic)   Mode 5   ♩. ♩.   (spondaic)

Mode 3   ♩. ♪♩   (dactylic)   Mode 6   ♪♪♪ ♪♪♪   (tribrachic)

Medieval notational symbols for these modes were selected from standard groupings of contiguous chant notes called ligatures; however, in varying circumstances one ligature could stand for rhythms in any one of several modes.

organum purum and discant

Polyphonic *organa* written in the style with rhythmic contrast in which only the upper, faster-moving voice was performed in flexible or modal rhythms, the notes of the bottom, *cantus-firmus*-bearing voice being extended into very long values, was called *organum purum.* Frequently notes of the bottom voice are so long that their vocal performance becomes exceedingly difficult, if not impossible. In such cases the bottom voice may have been performed on an instrument; of course, two soloists could allow their breathing to overlap and thus give the impression of long notes. The liturgical text originally belonging to the *cantus firmus* would be sung to the musical setting provided by the upper, added voice. (HAM, No. 28c and No. 29, *passim;* Fig. 18.)

When the other, more homogeneous type occurs, the voices are kept together by organizing both according to the rhythmic modes. Sections in one style may alternate with sections in the other. The style of a segment in which all rhythms are in the modes is called discant and the segment itself is called a *clausula.* A full stop usually occurs before and at the end of a *clausula,* which is thus a little independent section of polyphony in measured rhythm. (HAM, No. 28, d and e; No. 29, middle and near end.)

Perotin tended to turn away from *organum purum* in favor of discant style. In some cases he shortened many of Leonin's organa; in others he wrote completely new polyphony, a substitute *clausula,* to replace one by his predecessor. In many a *clausula* by Perotin there is a short rhythmic motive repeated throughout, such as:

Example 7. Typical repeated rhythmic pattern from a Parisian clausula, or motet.

Parisian clausula.

(HAM, Nos. 28d, e, h2, 30, and 31.)

An important achievement of Perotin was the extension of polyphony to three or four voices, although only four examples of the latter still survive. The name applied to the second voice of any polyphonic organum was *duplum;* the third melody line was called *triplum;* the fourth *quadruplum.* (HAM, No. 31; Omn, p. 15f; GlE, p. 36ff; AM-H, No. 5a.)

polyphonic conductus

Polyphonic *conductus* differed from polyphonic *organum* in two important ways. In the first place, as we have seen, the texts of conductus were rhymed lines in poetic meters. Second, all the music was newly composed, not written on a pre-existent *cantus firmus*. Polyphonic *conductus* was, therefore, the first artistic polyphony newly composed in its entirety. Furthermore, the note values in all voices — as many as four — were quite similar, resulting in a very homogeneous texture with motion almost note against note. Music of later generations, when its texture resembles this, is often said to be "in *conductus* style." (HAM, Nos. 38 and 39; Omn, p. 19; GIE, pp. 35, 41-44, 49; AM-H, Nos. 7-11.)

In Parisian polyphony the total range is very narrow and upper voices especially tend to lie in the same range, with much crossing of voices. There was often an exchange of the same passages between different voices, a practice called *Stimmtausch*. (HAM, No. 33a; GIE, p. 67.) Only the perfect octave, fifth, fourth, and unison were considered to be acceptable consonances on strong beats; in between, other intervals occur.

As we listen to this music we have a distinct disadvantage: it would be next to impossible for us ever to experience the same impact it had on the medieval congregation. To accomplish this we would have to banish every memory of any music that is not monolinear. Our ears are inured to complicated music — how could we ever successfully put ourselves in the place of the medieval worshippers to discover the thrill, the amazing novelty of hearing for the first time two or more melodies being sung simultaneously in one and the same composition! We have the further disadvantage that no modern phonograph could ever put us in the center of the deep, languid reverberation of the Gothic cathedral, the only place where the polyphonic Mass and motet are truly at home. We also lack the medieval religious consciousness, the so-called medieval mind, which would have thrilled not only to the new music reverberating but also to the enormous sense of union with the Divine in such a setting.

The Motet (Roach)(Max)

A discant *clausula*, being a closed section of polyphony, could be lifted out of its surroundings and performed independently of passages preceding and following it. In the early thirteenth century, perhaps sooner, it became the practice to add a new text to the upper voice of a *clausula*. The newly worded voice was then called *motetus* (Fr. *mot*, "word"). There were two essential characteristics of the thirteenth-century motet: (1) it was constructed on a *cantus firmus*, some pre-existent melody, (2) it had at least two different texts.

At first the new text was a Latin paraphrase of the original liturgical one belonging with the *cantus firmus*. The piece could be performed this way as part of the liturgy or independent of it. If the motet had three or four voices, new paraphrases might eventually be provided for each of these so that four different but related texts might be sung in one piece. But the original plainsong text, being usually very short, might then be omitted and the bottom voice played on an instrument, especially when the piece was performed apart from its liturgical surroundings. Eventually the new texts were not necessarily paraphrases and any interconnection could be subtle or nonexistent.

Next, the motet, being already polyphonic, polyrhythmic, and poly-textual, became also polyglot: one or more vernacular (French) texts might be substituted for Latin ones. Sacred at first, they soon became secular. Finally, composers might write a new melodic line to be sub-stituted for the one containing the *cantus firmus*, thus destroying all connection with the liturgy. Eventually they wrote entirely new music, some based on completely secular melodies, even street cries. The title of any motet is a composite of the text *incipit* from each of the voices, such as *O mitissima — Virgo — Hec dies*. (HAM, Nos. 28f, g, h2, i, 32, 33; Omn, p. 18f; P & O, No. 10; ParT, Nos. 10, 11, 12; GlE, pp. 58-69; AM-H, No. 5b; ML, V-5.)

Manuscript Sources

Four principal manuscripts preserve the early Parisian repertory, be-ginning with the music of Leonin's time. Two are now in the library at Wolfenbüttel, Germany (Fig. 14), but one of these was discovered in St. Andrews, Scotland. The third manuscript is in Florence, the fourth in Madrid. It is evident this music was known over a wide area, far from its point of origin. Sources important for the motet are the Montpellier codex, the Bamberg codex, and the Las Huelgas codex.

Polyphony was written at first in score notation, similar to the method used in modern music printing. However, it soon became evident that expensive parchment was being wasted when the bottom voice had only a few notes, thus needing very little space. Greater economy was realized even in some fascicles of early sources when scribes adopted choirbook format, with the *superius* (top voice), *contratenor* (middle voice), and tenor parts spread over one or two pages as shown in Example 8 and Figure 23. During the thirteenth century the five-line staff became standard in writing polyphony.

Example 8.   Representative arrangements of voices in choirbook format.

Drawing by Robert B. Green.

Before 1300 precision of notation was considerably improved by Franco of Cologne, who assigned values to modal notational symbols so certain combinations always had the same rhythmic equivalent. The rhythmic modes had been the basis of all notation for about a hundred and fifty years. The tyranny was broken when composers of the late thirteenth century, such as Pierre de la Croix, began to subdivide the semibreve into as many as seven parts and to place duple meter on a basis nearly equal to that of ternary. Typical were motets in which the superius was the fastest-moving voice, the contratenor somewhat slower, and the tenor slowest of all. (HAM, Nos. 34 and 35; AM-H, No. 12.)

THE AGE OF ISORHYTHMIC MUSIC

Important to us as a source for contemporary motets is the *Roman de Fauvel,* a literary work, dated 1316, which criticizes vices and abuses of the times. Fauvel, the name of a symbolic horse, is an acrostic derived from the initials of the vices *Flaterie, Avarice, Vilanie, Variété, Envie,* and *Lascheté.* Inserted in the narrative were about one hundred thirty pieces of music, including thirty-three motets. (HAM, No. 43; GIE, pp. 77-79.) Some of these antedated Franco, but the texts of later ones shared in the criticism aimed at abuses by the clergy and at corruption in other high places, such as the trial of the Order of the Templars by Philip the Fair to justify his seizure of their property.

The motets in this later group are organized musically in accordance with a technique to which the early twentieth-century historian Friedrich Ludwig applied the term *isorythm.* This technique was a culmination of a development from very small-scale beginnings in the bottom voice of many a Parisian polyphonic *clausula* that was organized in little repeated rhythmic or melodic patterns. (HAM No. 28d and e and Example 7.)

Gradually, these patterns grew in length and complexity until they culminated in isorhythm and isomelody which dominated musical style in fourteenth-century motets and was still used by prominent composers into the fifteenth century. In the system of isorhythm a composer arbitrarily selected a purely rhythmic pattern called a *talea* that might be very long and complicated. He applied this *talea* to the notes of a *cantus firmus*, usually a fragment of chant, called in terms of this technique the *color*. By intention the length of the *talea* did not match that of the *color*, in fact, the composer might have to repeat the *color* in order to extend its notes throughout the full length of the *talea*. Essentially this technique was applied in the tenor, but similar procedures were sometimes followed in one or all the upper voices as well. When either *talea* or *color* terminated, the same pattern began anew as many times as the composer wished. The last repetition of a *talea* might halve its previous rhythmic values. (HAM, No. 43; No. 44 and GIE, p. 88ff, are both isorhythmic and isomelic.)

Philippe de Vitry

Two brilliant people who wrote isorhythmic music shine forth with outstanding musical and intellectual achievements in the fourteenth century. First was Philippe de Vitry (1291-1361), probably from the province of Champagne, who soon became a member of the clergy and was elected Bishop of Meaux in 1351. Established at court as a leading royal officer, he rose to a position of great honor and achieved fame and distinction in political missions. His learning was most comprehensive. Only a torso of his music, a bare dozen compositions, has been preserved.

Philippe is best known as the author of a treatise called *Ars nova*, a term he originated to promote his novelties of style — in contrast to those of the late thirteenth century which he called the *Ars antiqua*. To him has been attributed the invention of the four prolations, which made possible a systematic duple or ternary division of all note values and gave equal importance to both. It is evident he was a master of the isorhythmic motet. (SchrP, Vol. I.)

The Polyphonic Mass

Isorhythm and isomelody figured prominently in the first examples of the polyphonic Mass, a category new in the late Middle Ages and destined to become one of the most important in the Renaissance. Under this term we understand polyphonic settings for the five parts of the Ordinary: Kyrie, Gloria, Credo, Sanctus and Benedictus, and Agnus Dei. In some of the fourteenth-century Masses part of the closing formula of the Mass, *Ite, missa est*, also is set to polyphony.

Although it was a prevailing custom in late medieval manuscripts to group together monophonic Kyries, Glorias and so forth, cycles of unified monophonic Ordinaries were known as early as the thirteenth century (*Missa de Angelis*). Thus, the cyclic Ordinary originated within monophonic chant, not as a result of imitating polyphonic Ordinaries.

Five polyphonic cycles, not all of them complete, are known in fourteenth-century music:

Mass of Tournai
Mass of Toulouse
Mass of the Sorbonne
Mass of Barcelona
Mass of our Lady, by Guillaume de Machaut

Of these, the Mass of Tournai is probably the oldest — at least, certain parts of it are. It is the first complete polyphonic Ordinary that has come down to us. Not all movements were by the same composer. The Ite is an isorhythmic motet.

Even in these early examples of the form are features that became standard practice in polyphonic Masses throughout the Renaissance — for example, the division of the Gloria by a full stop in the music just preceding the *Qui tollis*, and the soloistic performance by the priest of the first text phrases of both Gloria and Credo, after which the polyphony begins. Very unusual and interesting, however, are three examples of parody technique, a stylistic trait normally associated with music of the sixteenth century. In this method of composition the new polyphony, instead of being based on a monophonic *cantus firmus*, draws on all the voices of a pre-existing polyphonic model, each voice of which is parodied by the corresponding voice in the new composition. (SchrP, Vol. I; Agnus, ParT, No. 13.)

The harmonic successions — one cannot speak of "progressions" in the modern sense — in these works still sound awkward to our ears. Parallelism of voices and abrupt pauses in rhythmic flow, among other things, reflect a coldness that did not disappear from continental polyphonic writing until after the beginning of the fifteenth century. They are present in the most important polyphonic Mass of the fourteenth

century, the first which we know was written in its entirety by one
man: the *Mass of Our Lady* by Machaut.

Guillaume de Machaut

We notice immediately that his Mass is written for four voices. This
is noteworthy when we consider the first four Masses on the list are *a 3*
and trilinear music was still the norm for the times.

In this work Machaut employs a little formula which
acts as a unifying device. It also occurs with varying frequency, at
the same and other pitches, and in the same and other forms (often
the last note is missing), even in inversion, in Masses mentioned above:
in the Gloria of the Tournai Mass in the superius and the tenor, in the
Kyrie and Sanctus of the Toulouse Mass, and many times in the Mass
of Barcelona. One cannot help wondering whether Machaut consciously
turned to it for purposes of unity or whether its presence may simply
reflect a habitual, spontaneous occurrence of what has been aptly called
"coin of the realm:" melodic turns or fragments that pop up frequently
in the music of an era, nothing more than stylistic quirks in the very ink,
so to speak, of contemporary composers. Other formulas appear in
similar applications in Renaissance music.

The Kyrie, Sanctus, Agnus, and Ite of Machaut's Mass are in contemporary motet style — a very flexible texture in which the text phrases
do not occur simultaneously throughout the voices but tend to overlap.
Each of these movements is isorhythmic, with a *cantus firmus* from
plainsong, so each in itself is an isorhythmic motet. The upper two voices
tend to group themselves together in a style contrasting with that of the
lower pair.

The Gloria and Credo are in conductus style: the music is in a note-
against-note motion that is very chordal. The texts are set syllabically.
The greater length of these makes a more melismatic treatment imprac-
tical whenever the time needed for performance of a Mass must be considered. (SchrP, Vol. III; Kyrie, Omn, p. 20ff; Agnus I, P & O, No. 13;
GlE, p. 97f; ML, V-6.)

The question of instrumental participation in the performance is
raised by the presence of very short passages without text. It is believed
that instruments, especially brasses, customarily doubled vocal rendition
of melodic lines in the performance of polyphonic Masses, playing along
continuously as the choir sang, even though they are not called for in
the sources. Otherwise, these short, isolated passages without text, as in
the Machaut Mass, would be difficult to explain. The visual arts furnish
plenty of evidence to support this belief.

Machaut was the second great composer of the century. He was highly esteemed in his own time and remained in the memory of the French long after his death. He was very versatile — in fact, music was not his main occupation. He took holy orders when very young and was hardly more than twenty when he became secretary to John, King of Bohemia and Duke of Luxembourg. He traveled extensively, even after becoming canon of Rheims about 1356. He was significant as a poet, literary man, and diplomat. His works were collected under his own direction: he had scribes copy his music and poetry.

machaut's shorter compositions

Of his twenty-three remaining motets, twenty are isorhythmic, sometimes in the upper voices as well as in the tenor. Their length and complexity reveal forcefully the ingenuity of the composer.

It may seem strange that Machaut also wrote monophonic musical settings for poems, in forms used by contemporary composers of monody: *lais*, which are strophic, the first and last stanzas having the same music, and virelais, which he called *chansons balladées*. His polyphonic ballades are the earliest that have survived.

Of his polyphonic *rondeaux*, the best known is *Ma fin est mon commencement, et mon commencement ma fin* ("My end is my beginning, and my beginning my end"). The music of this very special three-voiced rondeau is so constructed that the notes of the B section consist of the notes of the A section in reverse order, with some exchange of parts:

A Section	B Section
Superius notes of the A section	noitces A eht fo seton ronetartnoC
Contratenor notes of the A section	noitces A eht fo seton suirepuS
Tenor notes of the A section	noitces A eht fo seton roneT

Composers about this time began to show much fondness for such musical trucks, puzzles, and various types of canon. (HAM, Nos. 44, 45, and 46; Omn, p. 23f; GlE, pp. 80-96; VHMS, Vol. III.)

Cadences and Musica Ficta

In the music of Machaut and other composers of the fourteenth century we find examples of a melodic cadential formula which, in a number of variants, usually in the top voice, was a favorite until late in the fifteenth century. Its identifying mark was a skip from the note a third under the *finalis* directly to that note at the cadence (6-8), in-

stead of by degreewise motion through the leading tone (6-7-8). For
this reason we call it the under-third cadence (Example 9a). Most harmonic cadences until at least the middle of the fifteenth century involved
in some application or other the degreewise outward motion from a sixth
to an octave position of two *finales* (Example 9b), or the inversion of
this, a third moving inward to a unison on one *finalis*. The under-third
melodic cadence, when applied to this harmonic motion, acted as an
embellishment (Example 9c).

Example 9.   Types of cadence formations.

a.   Dorian   Mixolydian   Phrygian

b.

c.

The foregoing examples show these various formulas notated strictly
according to three ecclesiastical modes, still the basic material for composition. But changes that take place in all phases of the arts originate
in man's desire to produce something that better pleases his senses, and
the ears of musicians of the late Middle Ages and the Renaissance were
more satisfied when performers applied certain inflections to the notes
of at least one voice in harmonic cadential formulas. They noticed the
stronger pull exerted toward the eighth degree of the mode when the
note approaching it from below is only a half step instead of a whole
step away. Thus, whenever a sixth moved to an octave or a third to a
unison at any cadence a chromatic inflection was often made in performance even though it was not indicated in the manuscript. The
singers understood as a part of performance practice just when and how
to carry out these chromatic changes. The inflections involved notes not

on the Guidonian hand, which to contemporary musicians were the only correctly available musical material. Because of this point of view they called these inflected notes *musica ficta,* or "artificial music." *Musica ficta* was not applied to cadences in the Phrygian mode (See Example 10).

**Example 10.   Example 9 as it would be
with musica ficta added.**

Inasmuch as performers of those times knew as part of their training just how to use *musica ficta,* very few written directions remain to guide us nowadays in making transcriptions. At those points where it seems most likely that degree inflections were added during performance a modern editor will usually either place a sharp, flat, or natural above the note in question — not, as is usually done, in front of it — or enclose these signs in parentheses, or both.

ITALIAN MUSIC OF THE LATE MIDDLE AGES

Because the under-third melodic cadence occurred frequently in the music of the Italian Francesco Landini (c.1325-97), it used to be called the Landini cadence. However, this cadence did not originate with him — in fact, it ornaments French music in the time of Machaut and before.

Composers in fourteenth-century Italy became active around 1325. The list includes a large number of men mostly of minor importance whose sacred music is of less interest to us than their secular pieces.

Many of them are associated with Florence: Giovanni da Florentia (or Firenze, also with the surname da Cascia, near Florence), Paulo da Firenze, Ghirardello da Firenze, Donato da Firenze, Lorenzo da Firenze, and Andrea da Firenze. With the exception of Giovanni (who antedates the others), these were in the second generation of a long list of metropolitan composers. Jacopo da Bologna, of the first generation, was the teacher of Francesco Landini, the most distinguished of the fourteenth-century group in Italy. In spite of having been blind from early childhood Landini became skilled as a player of several instruments.

The Ballata

The Italians used a form we first encountered by a different name in French secular monody. We have known as the virelai a piece whose sections were arranged in the order *AbbaA*, but the Italians called the same form a *ballata* — not to be confused with the French ballade, *aab(C)*. A section or two of a ballata occasionally lacks text, suggesting instrumental performance in those places. This factor, as well as its very name indicates that the ballata, too, was a dance piece at sometime in its history. (HAM, Nos. 51 and 53; Omn, p. 24; GlE, pp. 103-5.)

The Caccia

An even more strenuous and adventuresome activity is the subject of pieces in a second category favored by these Italian composers: the hunt, or *caccia* in Italian. The idea of the chase is easily depicted in music by the use of a canon, of which the *dux*, or leader, is pursued all the way to the end by the *comes*, the voice that follows the same melodic course as the *dux*, usually at a fixed time interval all the way. The name caccia was given to the trilinear Italian form in which the two upper voices, in canon, were accompanied by a third, lower voice that was independent of the others, provided harmonic support, and was frequently instrumentally performed. The single text, supplied for both voices of the canon, usually related details of a hunt or some other activity in daily life. The music is in two sections: all three voices come to a stop at a full cadence, whereupon a second, shorter canon with its third supporting voice brings the piece to an intense, exciting close. The second one is called a *ritornello*, a term applied to the final, short closing section of this and other musical forms. It had a function that might be compared to the *envoi* in French poetry. (HAM, No. 52; Omn, p. 25ff; GlE, p. 100ff.)

The Madrigal

Similar in basic plan to the caccia — a long, main portion followed by a short ritornello — was the madrigal. Its first appearance was as a fourteenth-century form. The origin of the term may be related either to its subject matter — *mandrialis*, a rustic, pastoral poem; or to its being written in the vernacular or mother tongue — *matricalis*, belonging to the womb. Normally it consisted of as many as four stanzas, each arranged in seven- or eleven-syllable lines, followed by a ritornello of two lines with new music occurring only at the end. (HAM, Nos. 49, 50 and 54; GIE, pp. 99, 106-17.)

Figure 15. Francesco Landini playing a portative organ and surrounded by several other instruments as depicted on the first page of his compositions in the Squarcialupi codex. (Courtesy of Biblioteca Medicea Laurenziana, Florence.)

The caccia, with its texture consisting of a pair of voices supported by a third, lower, often instrumental one, is a good representative of what might be called *duo-dominated* style. On the other hand, that texture *a 3* in which there is a soloistic, top vocal line supported by a pair of lower and possibly instrumental voices whose styles tend to match stylistically, has been called the *treble-dominated* style.

MUSICAL INSTRUMENTS

Landini and twelve other composers are represented with many ballatas, caccias, and madrigals in the largest and most beautifully illuminated manuscript containing fourteenth-century music, the Squarcialupi codex. The famous composer himself is depicted surrounded by various instruments. Among them is the lute, an instrument of eastern origin (Arab., el-'ud) known in Mesopotamia as early as 2000 B.C. Outstanding characteristics are its piriform body and the sharp angle of its pegbox (Figure 32). Many names and shapes characterized the psaltery, a very popular string instrument of the zither type, which was plucked by the fingers or with a plectrum. Very similar was the dulcimer, the main difference being that its strings were struck with curved beaters or padded sticks. The western harp, unlike most oriental varieties, had a pillar to complete the three sides of the frame; in late medieval times a small size was common. The lira (also lyra) illustrated in Figure 16 furnishes an example of the confusion in terms that often plagues the historian: this is a piriform bowed instrument of near eastern origin. Another form of bowed lyre developed into the Welsh crwth (pron., crōōth).

Of the bowed string instruments the most bizarre was the tromba marina, or nun's fiddle (Ger., *Trumscheit*) with a long, tapering, triangular body and frequently shown being played upside down over the shoulder. One leg of the bridge, extending through a sound hole and resting on the inside of the back, bore the main weight of the single string; the other, shorter leg was free to drum rapidly on the top of the instrument. The hurdy-gurdy was a fiddle-shaped instrument that was mechanically bowed: the player turned a crank which carried a rosined wheel extending up underneath the strings just in front of the bridge. The strings were stopped by key rods worked by the fingers of the left hand. The piriform rebec looked like some forms of the vielle; however, a basic difference was that the pegs, as in a modern violin, were in a line horizontal with the surface of the belly.

A popular wind instrument was the *cornetto* (Engl., cornett[1]), known in Germany as the Zink. Originally an animal's horn with holes, it was

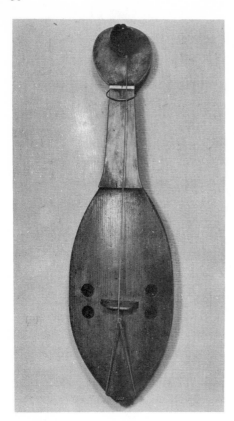

Figure 16. Lira, reproduction from sculpture in the portal of the Abbey of Moissac (twelfth century). (Courtesy of the Instrument Museum, Brussels.)

later made of wood and played with a cup-shaped mouthpiece: a tapering stick (often curved) was split, carved out, glued together, provided with finger holes, and covered with leather. The brass trumpet was often S-shaped. Not having valves, many specimens were provided with a very long mouthpiece that acted as a slide, thus enabling the player to reach tones between the natural partials. The trombone may not have been in use before the fifteenth century. Known in England as the sackbut, its tubing was thicker and its bore more conical than those of today, hence it had a mellower tone. A double-reed instrument, ancestor of the oboe, was the shawm or pommer. Flutes of both types, end blown (recorder) and side blown, were widely used.

Often depicted are two types of organs that could be carried about. The portative was small enough to be managed by one person with the help of a neck strap: the left hand worked a small bellows while the

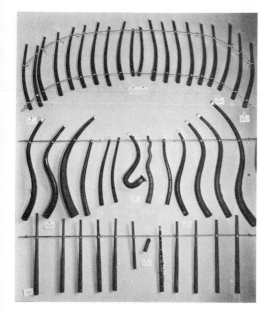

Figure 17. A collection of cornetts. (Courtesy of the Instrument Museum, Brussels.)

Figure 18. Musical instrument shop. In the foreground, left to right: positive organ, harp, trombone, drums, lute case, tromba marina; on the table: krummhorn, recorders, shawm, transverse flute, clavichord, and guitar. (Courtesy of the Metropolitan Museum of Art, Dick Fund.)

Die geschicklheit in der musiken und was in seinen ingenien und durch in erfunden und gepessert worden ist.

right operated the short keyboard. The positive was big enough to require its being placed (Lat., *positus*) on a table; one person in addition to the player was needed to work the bellows from behind the instrument.

A famous organ at Winchester, England is described in a poem by Wolfstan, who died in 963. Struck by his description of the "deafening sound" of this instrument, supplied with air by bellows worked by "seventy strong men," reliable historians have been misled into believing this must have been a monster unique in its era. However, careful evaluation of the single source for this information has shown that the Old Minster, Saxon predecessor of the present Norman Cathedral built in the late eleventh century, could not possibly have been large enough to house such a roaring dragon.

MEDIEVAL MUSIC IN ENGLAND

Although it is believed that Bernard de Ventadorn may have spent some time in England, there is very little evidence that the art of French secular monody had any influence there. Perhaps the oldest songs in the English language are those of St. Godric, a cave-dwelling hermit of the mid-twelfth century. There is also a group of monophonic songs that have rather stern, moralizing texts, such as *Worldes blisce ne last no throwe.* (HAM, No. 23; Omn, p. 14.)

Polyphony *a 2* in Britain was recorded by the late twelfth or early thirteenth century. We have no indication of exactly what is meant in that literary reference, but a thirteenth-century manuscript brings us a *Hymn to St. Magnus,* patron saint of the Orkney Islands. It is almost a kind of parallel organum, being written for two voices that move in parallel thirds throughout most of the piece, crossing occasionally through a unison (HAM, No. 25c; GIE, p. 47.)

Contemporary British sources bring us more polyphony in this style — later called *gymel* from a Latin word meaning "twin" — together with other examples showing influence of the continental style with its emphasis on perfect consonances. The first known motet with English text, *Worldes blisce — Domino,* contains passages in gymel style, as do examples of polyphonic conductus in late medieval British manuscripts. British composers particularly delighted in the fuller sonority of thirds and sixths — perhaps it was not entirely a case of chauvinism when Anonymous IV commented that the English "could sing delightfully."

The Summer Canon

Stimmtausch, mentioned above in connection with motets, is also a British trait — it may even have had its origin in England. One of the most famous examples is the *rota* (round) *Sumer is icumen in,* discovered on a leaf consigned to ignominious duty as part of the binding of a later volume. It is in the rhythmic modes and consists of two canons that proceed simultaneously. One of these is in four voices and carries the main text; the other is a two-voiced burden written in the *Stimmtausch* technique, with a simple refrain text. Thus, it is the first-known piece in six voices, although the occurrence of numerous unisons reduces the total number of pitches sounding at any one time. (HAM, No. 42; Omn, p. 17f; GIE, p. 45.)

English Six-three Technique

The fourteenth-century Worcester fragments, assembled from old bindings and wrappers of later manuscripts found in Worcester, Bodleian (Oxford), and British Museum libraries, indicate the presence, at Worcester in the fourteenth century of a group of composers whose works show both French and British influence. An *Alleluia psallat* is in *Stimmtausch* style for about three-quarters of its length. (HAM, No. 57a; SteM, p. 10ff.) The Worcester fragments reveal that British composers had an early liking for conductus style.

Many passages written in this style are trilinear, and chords are often arranged in thirds and sixths in the structure known as the $\frac{6}{3}$ chord, or the first inversion of a triad in root position. Parallel motion in thirds and sixths extends over passages of varying length. The *cantus firmus* appears in either the bottom or the middle voice. Included in the Worcester fragments are a number of polyphonic settings of tropes for the Mass in which this technique is present. One trilinear Gloria preserved there is largely based on it; passages are introduced and quitted in typical fashion, with bare chords consisting of root, fifth, and octave. (HAM, No. 57b.) The British composers' delight in fullness of sound, exemplified in this style, is one of the outstanding characteristics of their music, destined to have an effect on the style of later continental music.

Polyphonic Mass Compositions

Composers working in the British Isles included Leonel Power, Damett, Cooke, and Typp. Many of their compositions are preserved

Figure 19. Minstrels' Gallery, about 1340, Cathedral at Exeter, England. Nos. 1, 2, 3, 4, 5, 7, 9, and 11 (l. to r.) are a cittern, bagpipes, cornett (?), fidel, harp, trumpet, portative organ and tambourine. Although the lute is not known in English literature until about 1395, No. 9 appears to have a bent-back pegbox and to be played with a plectrum, but the shape of the body is not characteristic. The other instruments are broken. (Courtesy of the Dean and Chapter of Exeter Cathedral.)

in a most important and beautiful collection called the Old Hall manuscript, containing pieces believed to have been written about the turn of the fifteenth century. This source shows that the English were very active in writing polyphonic settings of the Ordinary. However, in Old Hall there is no sign of an effort to create a full, unified setting of the usual five sections. Furthermore, there are no settings for the Kyrie in Old Hall nor did it become practice for British composers to provide polyphonic settings for this text until late in the sixteenth century. In this source polyphonic Glorias are grouped together, as are also settings for the Credo, Sanctus, and Agnus. Of ninety-seven polyphonic Mass sections, seventy-six are for three voices; one is *a 6*, nine *a 5*, and eleven *a 4*. Pieces in conductus style precede those in a later motet style. Although in many of the settings the number of voices does not change, in several examples there are fewer for certain portions of the text. Sometimes changes in meter occur as new sections begin. There are examples of canon, early occurrences of points of imitation (see below, p. 83), and introductory duos. These traits are continued and become firm custom in many polyphonic Masses throughout the Renaissance.

Another even more important set of sources contains music by English composers of this era. Seven manuscripts discovered in Trent, Italy contain altogether about fifteen hundred pieces by composers all over western Europe, many of them by the same Englishmen represented in Old Hall. In these Trent manuscripts are many works by the most influential British composer of the early fifteenth century, John Dunstable. It is interesting that the most important sources for Dunstable's work are those originating outside England. His music helped transform the style of contemporary and later continental composers and will be discussed in the next chapter.

SOURCES AND ADDITIONAL READINGS

ApF	DiF	MarD	SchrM
AuC	EaH	NO	SchrP
BaS	FeH	PiH	SmH
BessM	HarMB	RamO	StäF
BraI	HayR	ReMMA	UrC
BukM	KeW	RiE	WagM
BukS	KiP	SaH	WaiR
CouM	MacM	SchrF	WolE

LISTENING ASSIGNMENTS

1. P & O, No. 9; ParT, No. 9. Classify under heading of *organum purum* or discant.
2. P & O, No. 10; ParT, No. 10. What comments may be made about the bottom voice of each?
3. P & O, No. 12. Outline the form. How are sections musically related?
4. ParT, No. 13. In what style is this Agnus? What cadence type predominates?
5. P & O, No. 13. Notice isorhythmic patterns in the tenor and contratenor.
6. PartT, No. 16. In what style is this piece? What is the musical relation between the two upper voices? What name is applied to the section in 3/4 time?
7. *VHMS*, Vol. II: Early polyphony, the Summer Canon, medieval dances. For other pieces in HAM and Omn, see record list.

WRITTEN ASSIGNMENTS

1. Look at the music of P & O, Nos. 7 and 8. Which intervals are generally regarded as consonances (occurring when both voices move)? In No. 8, do you think you might recognize the *cantus firmus* as a melody just from hearing the piece? Why?

2. Study HAM, Nos. 26c, 27a, and 29. How was early polyphony performed (see text, p. 49)?

3. Find the soloistic sections of HAM, Nos. 28d, 28e, and 29, of which all voices are in the rhythmic modes. What term is applied to these portions of the polyphony? What form originated in such passages?

4. What do you notice about the bottom voice of each motet in HAM, No. 32? What kind of motet developed from these stylistic traits?

5. What unusual features do you notice about the motets in HAM, Nos. 33a, 34, and 35?

6. What are the main differences between the pieces in HAM, Nos. 38 and 39, and examples of polyphonic organum you have examined?

7. What is the style of each of the following: HAM, Nos. 52, 54, and 57? Give reasons for your answers.

FOOTNOTES

[1]The spelling with two t's is used to differentiate this instrument from the more modern brass cornet.

the age of dufay

The Renaissance was a time of human awakening. In its literal meaning of "rebirth" it has frequently been called "the revival of learning," with reference to the influence of classical antiquity. But it would be better to speak of a new interest in culture, perhaps a rebirth of human spirit, even a rebirth of Italian spirit after many centuries of barbarian thought. However, there was no "rebirth" in music, so we speak of "music in the Renaissance," not "the Renaissance of music."

No one would wisely dispute the importance of the rediscovery of ancient literature. The fall of Constantinople in 1453 caused many learned men to flee to the west, taking with them copies of classic volumes known to comparatively few people west of Greece. But Petrarch (1304-74), the first outstanding man of letters of the Italian Renaissance, had already been acquainted with Latin translations. The more general recovery of ancient art and literature was only one of the generative impulses of the Renaissance.

WANING STRENGTH OF THE CHURCH

A second factor was the break in the power of the church in the fourteenth century. The church had been the dominating force in the lives of most people for more than a thousand years, ever since the acceptance and recognition of the Christian religion by Constantine. It had watched over them from baptism to requiem. The power of the church in wealth and politics had grown to such an extent that it did not just equal but even exceeded that of the state. With its large amount of ecclesiastical and worldly property it took care of both spiritual and secular obligations. Officials of the church constituted a sharply defined class. They occupied the highest rank of society, called the first estate; the second estate embraced the nobility; the commoners formed the third estate.

However, as civil states gained in strength, conflicts between them and the church grew in frequency and proportion. Christian theory affirmed that both church and state derived from God, represented by the Pope in one case and the emperor in the other. But the Pope had brushed aside the idea of equality and made the church superior so the emperor and all other civil rulers actually kept their positions subject to his approval.

Civil resentment and criticism, aroused by abuses with which we have become familiar and which had been smouldering for many decades, now flared into the open. Though critics were quickly branded heretics and even burned at the stake, the rebellion could not be put down.

RISE OF THE BURGER CLASS

A third factor contributing to the life pattern of Renaissance man was the urbanization already mentioned. This, plus the founding of more universities and the weakening of the church, gave rise to one of the important goals of the Renaissance: liberation from restraining bonds and inhibitions that characterized the thinking of the Middle Ages.

But the universities did not affect the rising burger, who wanted sanction for new worldly ways. Partly as a result of Petrarch's interest, Latin became not merely a language taught in universities as a tool for dry learning but also a portal to that fresh and genial outlook on life called humanism. The revival of interest in culture that is integral with humanism came from Renaissance man's desire to find authority, or at least example and excuse for his worldliness. Men went back to ideas and institutions of the ancient world to find principles they could substitute for those formerly provided by the church. To generations emerging from medievalism, classical antiquity also brought instruction in the art, morals, philosophy, and science of Greece and Rome.

The Crusades, too, had helped create in the minds of Western men an interest in the rest of mankind. The new awareness of worldly affairs — secularization — became a prominent trait of Renaissance man. The world and the beauties that fill it absorbed and monopolized human consciousness. But the fullest possible enjoyment of worldly beauties is not possible without abundant means with which to provide them.

NEW WEALTH THROUGH COMMERCE

A fifth and indispensable factor without which the Renaissance in the arts would not have been possible was the acquisition of new wealth. By 1100, Chinese silk and spices were the delight of wealthy Mohammedans in the Levant. Their beautiful clothes of silk and brocade, decorated with gold and silver threads, and their many sumptuous artifacts in gold and ivory had excited the envy of Italian traders. Spices, too, assumed tremendous significance. The Italians made these luxuries avialable to the west and north. In exchange, they brought back elegant furs, linen, wool, and timber obtained from the north and thus set up a trade that made them and their native city-states extremely affluent.

Before 1250, trade routes to China had been over land, but these were diverted by conquests of the Mongols. They were fierce fighters; they had a superior kind of armor made of boiled leather; and they used Chinese gunpowder to scare the horses of Western warriors. Merchants, therefore, had to find new routes — by water. Ever since the late twelfth century, long voyages had been made easier by two vital improvements in the science of navigation: the development of the mariner's compass and the transformation of the steering oar into the rudder.

For sea trade, Italy was particularly favored. Some of her merchants went north over the Alps, up the Rhone valley, or through the Pillars of Hercules to trading points in France, Germany, England, Ireland, and Scotland to sell exotic finery and bring back northern products. Their profits were fattened by mushrooming sales — especially of pepper.

Pepper became an important financial commodity. To the western nobleman and burger it became a luxury, its possession a status symbol. This was its chief importance. Only secondary was its use as a mask to cover the taste of meat no longer fresh because of lack of refrigeration. Italian merchants obtained their spices and other exotic rareties from Alexandria. The monopoly thus held by Alexandria and Italy (especially Venice) caused a rise in the price of pepper. This induced countries to the west of Italy to seek new trade routes to the east — hence the geographical explosion of Europe, led by Spain and Portugal.

Burgundy

Various areas in northwest Europe also were enriched. One of these was Burgundy, which included within its boundaries in the fifteenth century a large part of central as well as western France. Its long history dates back to a people driven westward from northeastern Germany in the fifth century. Philip the Good, duke from 1419 to 1469, formed an alliance with England. In 1420 he acknowledged Henry V of England

Figure 20. View of Venice, woodcut by Erhardt Reuwich from Breyden-bach's Peregrinations (1486). Church of St. Mark's is in the center. (Courtesy of the Metropolitan Museum of Art, Rogers Fund, 1919.)

as king of France and shortly thereafter gave his sister in marriage to John, Duke of Bedford, brother of Henry. Bedford acted as regent of France after the death of Henry in 1422. Under Philip the Good and his son Charles the Bold the duchy flourished. It was able to support many artists such as painters, sculptors, musicians.

NEW PHASES IN THE ARTS

A rebirth of classical ideals of clarity, simplicity, and strictness of style revitalized architecture, sculpture, and painting. Of all the arts, architecture was influenced most by the revival of interest in forms of antiquity. The graceful column and lintel replaced the massive pier and flying buttress of the Gothic cathedral. Sculpture, too, not only revealed careful study of classical harmony of proportions but also sought faithful representation of reality, one goal of the Renaissance artist. Thus, statues by Claus Sluter, for example, look like a moment of frozen action in a living drama. Painting became more realistic through the application of new knowledge about the laws of perspective, extending new depth behind the flat surface of the canvas. New techniques involving the suspension of colors in oils and the use of minute brushes, especially in the hands of the Van Eyck brothers, made it possible to reproduce fine details with startling precision and exactness, infusing new life and sparkle into canvases of the Flemish and Italian masters: we can see the light in each eye, we can nearly count the hairs on animals, or follow the course of threads in lace.

But though ancient discipline greatly influenced literature and the visual arts, there was no comparable effect on music — no rebirth of ancient music. The new wealth enabled many a member of the European nobility to establish at his court a chapel staffed with musicians who furnished sacred music for his religious services and secular music for entertainment. A trickle of activity in widely scattered courts soon rose to a torrent in many, for the wealthier nobility could support a greatly increased demand for new music and composers. Thus began a system of patronage in which musicians until the end of the eighteenth century found their sole dependable livelihood in the courts of nobility, or under the auspices of the church or town. One of the chapels supporting brisk and vigorous creativity was at the court of Burgundy.

Figure 21. St. Gregory institutes the litanies during the plague, by the Limbourg brothers, from a Book of Hours (1410-13) belonging to the Duke of Berry, brother of Philip the Bold. (Courtesy of the Metropolitan Museum of Art, The Cloisters Collection, Purchase, 1954.)

THE PRINCIPAL COMPOSERS AND THEIR WORKS

In the entourage of the Duke of Bedford was an English astronomer, mathematician, and musician by the name of John Dunstable (c. 1380-1453). Because of the Duke's long residence in France, Dunstable was in extended contact with musical circles at the courts in Paris and Dijon, seat of the dukes of Burgundy. He may have visited Italy also. Through an often-quoted poem and by examination of stylistic traits in their music, we know he had a marked influence on native musicians at the Burgundian court: Martin le Franc in his *Le Champion des Dames* (c.1440) relates the shame and envy of Dufay and Binchois as they heard the characteristically English sonorities of Dunstable's compositions.

Guillaume Dufay (c.1400-1474), one of the earliest truly genial figures in the history of music, at least visited the Burgundian court; we do not know how long he may have resided there. He became a choirboy at Cambrai, where the cathedral was renowned for its music in the fifteenth century. From 1420 to about 1443 he seems to have spent most of his time in Italy, making intermittent trips back to his native country. We find his name included among those of the singers in the Papal choir in Rome. Following this, in the mid-1430s, he was in the ducal service at Savoy. We have various indications of the esteem in which he was held. For example, he was granted more than one prebend – stipends of the funds of a cathedral for the financial support of an individual – one having been from the cathedral at Cambrai. In this city he spent perhaps the last twenty years of his life, surrounded by pupils, contributing new works to musical repertoire, and enjoying the life of a personality of international renown.

Dufay's principal contemporary was Gilles de Binche, known as Binchois, born in Hennegau near Mons about 1400. After military service he may have visited England in the service of the Duke of Suffolk. He was soon located in Burgundy where he is recorded as having been court chaplain for most of the second half of his life. He died in 1460. He and Dufay are depicted togther in *Le Champion des Dames*.

NEW FEATURES OF STYLE

Martin le Franc's remarks in his poem may have been referring to the fullness of sound already mentioned. Curiously enough, it may have been on their trips to Italy that the northerners felt the greatest impact of English music, which so influenced the sound of their own compositions. For example, melodic lines when approaching a cadence frequently formed $\frac{6}{3}$ chords which moved degreewise downward one after the other until the last one cadenced on a bare chord consisting of an octave and a fifth. Thus, the two cadence chords were what we now call a VII₆-I progression. Generally the succession of $\frac{6}{3}$ chords was embellished, the top voice frequently having been decorated with some form of the under-third melodic cadence formula. In example 11a the two chords of a typical cadence are shown as they would appear in two of the ecclesiastical modes. We have seen that *musica ficta* was usually applied to the top voice if the two voices just before an octave were a minor sixth apart, though not if the cadence was a Phrygian one. Thus, when raised to a distance of a half step from the *finalis* of the mode, the note on the seventh scale degree in the top voice became a true leading tone. In trilinear polyphony Burgundian composers frequently applied *musica ficta* to the middle voice as well; a note there, too, when raised a half step, could become a leading tone to the note it preceded. The resulting formation is therefore a double-leading-tone cadence often called the Burgundian cadence (Example 11b). A sampling of methods

Example 11. Influence of $\frac{6}{3}$ technique in approaches to cadences.

in which the skeletal structure of the VII$_6$-I type of cadence was decorated in the fifteenth century is shown in Example 12.

In another cadential arrangement of voices the bottom voice of the
penultimate chord occupied the note a fourth below the *finalis,* and the
two upper voices were a sixth apart. The cadence was completed when

Example 12. Typical fifteenth-century cadence formations.

the sixth moved outward to the octave, as it did in the VII$_6$-I type, and
the bottom voice leaped upward an octave, crossing the bottom voice,
to the fifth of the final chord of the cadence (Example 13a). It will be
seen that this movement of voices resulted in the sound of a V-I cadence,
which was achieved when the voices moved to a tripled *finalis,* as in
Example 13b.

Normally, the texture in the fifteenth-century chanson consisted of
three voices, as in most earlier polyphony; however, four voices became
available when the contratenor, usually the middle voice, was split so
another voice, also called contratenor, took its position below that of
the tenor. The four voices, soon to become the prevailing texture in all
categories, then consisted (from to top bottom) of superius, *contratenor
altus* ("high contratenor"), tenor, and *contratenor bassus* ("low con-

Example 13.   Typical octave-leap and V-I cadences.

a.

b.

tratenor"). Composers could thus use a *cantus firmus* in the tenor and still manipulate the bottom voice freely in order to provide for the structure more sonority and a firm harmonic foundation of a bass line. The quadrilinear texture first became standard in polyphonic settings for the Ordinary of the Mass.

A most important new trend in style was one that may be traced to the influence of the caccia and other pieces that are, or contain, canons. In the early fifteenth century composers began more often to repeat the same melodic fragment, or motive, in different voices of polyphony. Thus, one or more voices imitated — not always exactly — melodic material that had just been heard elsewhere in the texture. The use of imitation gradually increased to the point, near the end of the century, where it became a form-producing element in itself. When imitation occurs throughout the texture every time a new voice enters, usually after a rest, the term *pervading imitation* becomes applicable. Each area in the texture where one motive is treated in this way is called a "point of imitation" (Example 14).

It seems that polyphony remained soloistic until about 1420. After that time manuscripts were larger so that more than two or three could

**Example 14.   Point of imitation at the beginning of Dufay's
ce jour de l'an.**

StaM, p. 102.

sing from them. Also, we begin to find in the music written indications
such as *Unus, Duo,* and *Chorus.*

Polyphonic Masses: Dunstable

Some Mass settings by Dunstable reflect the tendency to group movements in unified arrangements. A simple way of doing this was to use
the same *cantus firmus* for two or more Mass movements. A three-voiced
Gloria and Credo by Dunstable preserved in one of the Trent manuscripts are each based on the plainsong *Jesu Christi Fili Dei.* The *cantus
firmus* occurs twice in each movement in extended note values. A *Missa
Rex saeculorum,* attributed to Dunstable in one source and to Leonel
Power in another, unifies four movements of the Ordinary (the Kyrie
is missing, cf. p. 72) through use of the same *cantus firmus* in each
movement. To the latter composer is attributed another such cycle, the
M. Alma Redemptoris mater. This type of Mass, called the *cantus-firmus*
Mass (all movements based on the same *cantus firmus*), was a most
significant English contribution inasmuch as it was cultivated extensively
by important composers throughout the Renaissance.

the cantus firmus of polyphonic masses

The notes of the tenor of the *cantus-firmus* Mass were usually
disposed in extended time values; being thus less easily distinguishable
and harder to sing, they may have been given over entirely to instru-

mental performance. The vocal performance of the other voices was still supported, in all probability, by brass instruments.

If a composer took a *cantus firmus* from the Proper, performances of such a Mass would have to be limited to one annual liturgical occasion. Thus, probably to make possible the performance of a work more than once a year, he usually chose a tune that had no such seasonal limitations. But a secular melody would be much better in this respect, for it could not possibly have any liturgical connection at all. Therefore, he frequently took for a *cantus firmus* the tenor line of some secular polyphonic chanson, usually a contemporary favorite either by the same or another composer. Any Mass, whether based on a sacred or secular *cantus firmus*, acquired the name of that melody — thus, the *M. Ave Regina caelorum* was based on that Marian antiphon, and the *M. Se le face ay pale* by Dufay on the tenor of his own chanson by that name. (P & O, No. 15) A work called *M. sine nomine* may be one in which the composer wished to conceal the name of the *cantus firmus,* or it may be one to which no title is given in the source and whose *cantus firmus* is unknown to historians.

It may seem strange and frivolous that music intended for the most solemn service of the church could have such a profane point of departure, especially when one considers that a secular tune called *L'Homme armé,* whose text seems innocuous enough but probably has very vulgar implications, was used in this way more often than any other secular melody. However, the intent was only mischievous, not sacrilegious. Furthermore, the extending of the note values of the *cantus firmus* prevented the recognition of the tune by most hearers so the presence of a risqué meaning was probably not part of general knowledge. A possible reason for the frequent selection of *L'Homme armé* is that it is in ABA form, which is ideally suited for use in three-sectional Mass movements such as the Kyrie and Agnus. (HAM, No. 66a; Omn, p. 28.)

Dufay

Most of the foregoing features may be observed in the Masses of Dufay. His earliest compositions in this category, probably written before 1440, consist of single movements or pairs of movements, such as Gloria-Credo, with little or no musical relationship. In some of his early independent movements, plainsong and polyphonic sections alternate. Frequently they show the influence of English $\frac{6}{3}$ technique, but the *cantus firmus* occurs in the superius. We find verbal instructions, such as *Duo* and *Omnes,* reflecting the new tendency described above.

In one independent Gloria that paraphrases the Gloria of plainsong Mass IX in the superius, Dufay uses blocked chords held by fermatas to emphasize certain text words, a trick occurring in later compositions by him and other composers as well. In another Gloria (*De Quaremiaux,* for Lent) there is a ground bass: the same melody and rhythmic patterns are repeated.

Dufay's *Gloria ad modum tubae* is especially renowned. Here, too, there is an ostinato, pendulating back and forth between mostly tonic and dominant notes. Motives are shared in alternate performance by the two bottom voices of the quadrilinear texture, which may have been played by trumpets or sung by human voices in imitation of those instruments. The two upper voices are in canon.

dufay's complete masses

Three of Dufay's eight complete Masses probably belong in the period before 1440. Of these three, two are *a 3* and mostly in treble-dominated style. The last in this group, the *M. Sancti Jacobi,* is unusual in its inclusion of polyphonic settings for four parts of the Proper. Significant is the fact that its Communion is an early example of a continental style that may have sprung from English $\frac{6}{3}$ technique. In this new style only two voices, the top and bottom, are notated; inasmuch as the middle voice was always sung a perfect fourth below the top voice it was not necessary to write out the former. The composer needed only to place at the beginning of the passage, consisting of the two outer voices, the phrase *à fauxbourdon* to signify that the third voice should be added in performance. This style, called *fauxbourdon,* may have been a contribution of Dufay himself. (ML, V-8.)

His Cyclic Masses

Dufay's five later Masses (a sixth, the *M. La Mort de St. Gothard,* may also be his), all written probably after 1440, are of the new quadrilinear *cantus-firmus* type with the same *cantus firmus* in the tenor of each polyphonic movement. The tenor is often the last to enter, and anticipatory imitation of the *cantus firmus* frequently occurs as other voices make their entries. In many Mass sections of this and later generations the two upper voices are the first to enter, thus forming an introductory upper-voice duo. A short motive may be repeated at the opening of each movement. This is called a head-motive and may be in one voice or in as many as three, that is, in all except the tenor, the *cantus-*

firmus-bearing voice. These motives may involve anticipatory imitation of the *cantus firmus* or may simply be another case of "coin of the realm," perhaps originating from plainsong formulas.

Dufay's *M. Se le face ay pale,* one of this last group, typifies the Renaissance composer's love for puzzles. Instead of writing out all four parts, he provided only three and added verbal directions which, when correctly followed, showed how to sing the notes of the *cantus firmus* in order to make them fit those of the other voices. We call directions of this kind a *verbal canon,* the latter word being used in its original sense of "rule," or "law." (P & O, No. 15.)

Dufay's *M. L'Homme Armé* may be the first in about thirty Masses for which that tune was selected as *cantus firmus.* Its closing section, the Agnus III, involves another verbal canon: *Cancer eat plenus et redeat medius,* of which a full interpretation in this application might be, "Let the crab proceed forward in notes of full value and then let him come back in notes of halved time value." Inasmuch as crabs are assumed to move backward, the notes of the well-known melody must first be sung backward in the tenor. Then, since a backward motion by the crab would be what we consider motion forward, the notes must be sung throughout the remainder of the movement in normal order. But the time values of the notes during the second occurrence are to be only half as long as those in the first; hence, the melody (in reverse) is spread over two-thirds of the movement at first and over the last third (in normal order) on second hearing. (HAM, No. 66c.)

Certain parts of monophonic plainsong Ordinaries were customarily sung by a few soloists; in polyphonic Masses these same portions were often scored for fewer than the full number of voices. At least one voice, usually the tenor, was omitted so the *cantus firmus* was not heard during the performance of that section. Portions handled in this way were the Christe eleison, Benedictus, Pleni, and Agnus II. Various other segments, usually of the longer Gloria and Credo, were often treated as independent duos or trios.

The *cantus-firmus* Mass was at the height of its popularity in the late fifteenth century but appeared frequently during the next hundred years and beyond.

Motets and Other Sacred Music

Soon after 1400 the motet began to change. In the first decades of the fifteenth century isorhythm gradually disappeared. In France, the style of the motet, still based on a *cantus firmus* and still polytextual, was inclined to be conservative. However, in Italian motets of the same period, although there are some with isorhythm, new features are discernible. Many were freely composed, not being based on any pre-existent melody; there are motets in which imitation begins to appear as a form-producing element. Generally speaking, in the fifteenth and sixteenth centuries the motet is simply a freely composed polyphonic piece with a Latin scriptural text not from the Ordinary.

dunstable

Some of Dunstable's motets, mostly *a* 3, are isorythmic (ParT, No. 18); some employ the $\frac{6}{3}$ technique or demonstrate in other ways the English predilection for fullness of sound; others combine $\frac{6}{3}$ technique and more freely composed polyphony, totally independent of any pre-existent melody. Such a piece is *Quam pulchra es*, which well illustrates the English characteristics so often mentioned and the northern tendency to include thirds and triads in a melodic line. Hearing this work makes it easier to understand how the English influenced continental style and why Dunstable has been called the first "musical" composer. (SteM, p. 19ff.)

The superius of Dunstable's motet *Sancta Maria* opens with a motive that occurs in various rhythmic forms in fifteenth-century music — there are three more in the superius of this piece — and might thus qualify under the heading "coin of the realm." It resembles slightly the plainsong formula for the fifth mode, shown on page 30, and might have had its origin there. Another coin of perhaps similar minting, which becomes an ubiquitous cliché in several versions until the very end of the sixteenth century, also appears in the top voice of this piece. The melodic style of this composition, too, is quite triadic. Dunstable varies the musical color by introducing passages in which the two lower voices or the two upper voices appear as short duos. Rhythmic variety is present whenever the basic ternary measure is temporarily displaced by $\frac{6}{8}$ in one or all the voices, as in Example 15 and in the penultimate measure — a very frequent occurrence in Renaissance music. Several cadences show the influence of $\frac{6}{3}$ technique and varieties of the under-third melodic formula. (HAM, No. 62.)

dufay

Some of Dufay's motets, too, are isorhythmic but these are early ones. A beautiful motet (not isorhythmic) based on the *Alma Redemp-*

Example 15.   Metric changes in Duntable's Sancta Maria.

toris mater melody is in treble-dominated three-voiced texture. The Marian antiphon is paraphrased in the superius; the two other voices were probably played on instruments. The adaptation of the melody in the motet is artistically proportioned, with a long, stately, arched line, presenting a wide variety of rhythmic groupings treated with great flexibility. Blocked, fermata-held chords emphasize the text and reflect the calmness that can be the answer to a prayer in veneration of the Virgin. (HAM, No. 65. See also *Flos florum*, SteM, p. 14f.)

Numerous pieces, such as settings of the Magnificat, in which Dufay employs *fauxbourdon*, show how easily he assimilated English influence. In hymn settings he specifies *fauxbourdon* with the chant melody paraphrased in the top voice for the even-numbered stanzas, the odd-numbered ones to be sung to the original plainsong. (Omn, p. 27f.)

Dufay also wrote a number of sacred pieces with Italian texts, such as the lovely music for *Vergine bella*, a sonnet by Petrarch.

binchois

Binchois seems to have been less interested than Dufay in writing sacred music. Usually his settings of sacred texts are *a 3* and many of them are *fauxbourdon*-like. The application of its technique in his music for Psalm 113, *In exitu Israel*, amounts to little more than a trilinear harmonization of a psalm tone: two basic musical formulas in $\frac{6}{3}$ technique, applied alternately to the two halves of each psalm verse, are varied according to the demands of the text.

The Chanson

Binchois is at his best in the writing of polyphonic chansons. In this century the popularity of the virelai and ballade did not keep pace with that of the rondeau. A large proportion of fifteenth-century chanson texts overstate a playfully declaimed, melodramatic melancholy of love that is allegedly not returned by the object of adoration.

In most cases the *rondeaux* were longer and more complicated; when units of the basic eight-line structure, *ABaAabAB*, were doubled, the result was the *rondeau quatrain*: *ABCDabABabcdABCD*. In the *rondeau cinquain* lines were arranged *ABCDEabcABCabcdeABCDE*, the form of Binchois' *De plus en plus*. Many fifteenth-century chansons, like this one, have instrumental introductions, interludes, or postludes. *De plus en plus* illustrates several traits already discussed, such as treble-dominated style, the under-third melodic cadence formula, the octave-leap cadence (at the end of the first text line), the VII$_6$-I type of cadence approached by a passage influenced by $\frac{6}{3}$ technique (at the end), and the application of *musica ficta* (HAM, No. 69.)

Some chansons are not in the more common *formes fixes*. Binchois' *Filles à marier*, a light-hearted warning to bachelor girls that jealousy can destroy happiness in marriage, is in simple binary form. The upper two of its four voices are in canon, supported by two different instrumental lines. (HAM, No. 70.)

arnold and hugo de lantins

Arnold de Lantins and Hugo de Lantins, contemporaries of Binchois and Dufay, may or may not have been related — at least, both probably came from the town of Lantins in the province of Liège. A rondeau by Arnold, *Puisque je voy*, is rather clearly in treble-dominated style, in which the two lower voices frequently are in nearly the same range and cross one another freely as in this case. Here the range is f to f', with one of the voices going to g'. (HAM, No. 71.)

In music before the Baroque no bar lines are present in the sources. When bar lines are added by modern editors and placed at regularly recurring intervals, this may destroy or at least conceal other metric arrangements that the composer or the contemporary performer might have had in mind. The music was probably performed with a rhythmic flexibility that is practically impossible to show when bar-lines are added according to the system in use over the past 250 years. For example, metric groupings in the B section of Arnold's rondeau might be viewed as in Example 16. Various meters appear, resulting in a more interesting and varied rhythmic texture in which $\frac{3}{4}$, $\frac{6}{8}$, $\frac{3}{2}$, and "$\frac{3 + 3 + 2}{8}$" (dochmiac) groupings follow or occur with or against similar or contrasting rhythmic arrangements.

Hugo's rondeau, *Ce ieusse fait*, appears at first to be in duo-dominated style; this is true at least in that points of imitation occur only between the two upper voices. But further examination of the style of each part shows there are stylistic similarities between the two lower

voices as well and there is more homogeneity than contrast in the texture as a whole. (HAM, No. 72.)

dunstable

Homogeneity and uniformity of style, although with great rhythmic
flexibility, are present to a large extent in Dunstable's *O Rosa bella.*
Imitation occurs even during the instrumental prelude. At the place
where the text begins, a point of imitation unifies all three melodic

Example 16.   Flexibility of meter in A. de Lantins' Puisque je voy.

lines — a foretaste of pervading imitation. A certain unity is given to
the piece through Dunstable's use of the interval of a fifth between
d′ and g: at the opening, the bare fifth is imitated in the bottom voice;
soon the same interval with intervening notes is heard in the superius;
it appears in triad formation with imitation, as we have seen, where the
text begins; later it is emphasized in other rhythms, especially in the
little arabesques of descending eighth notes of which the first is tied
to its preceding note. This little figure, by the way, is reminiscent of

the one occurring so frequently in fourteenth-century French Masses —
perhaps here, too, a case of "coin of the realm." Although most of this
chanson is in quadruple measure, it changes to $\frac{3}{4}$ near the end. Similar
occurrences are frequent in Renaissance music; the purpose is to speed
up the motion to effect a final climax with more tension in a livelier
passage, all of which produces a drive to the cadence. (HAM, No. 61.)

dufay

In chansons by composers in this generation we find that pieces in
ternary meter are still in vogue. Dufay's *Pouray je avoir votre merci*
opens with a point of imitation — a single motive occurs at the beginning
of each voice, much as in Example 14. There is no more imitation in
the rest of the chanson, however. Some imitation is also present in his
Adieu m'amour, a *rondeau cinquain*, notated in quadruple meter although a variety of metric groupings gives flexibility to the texture. Duo-
dominated style prevails. At the end of the A section there is a good
example of a Burgundian cadence with the under-third melodic cadence
formula in two of the voices. The postlude at the end is the only purely
instrumental section, although many of Dufay's chansons have an instrumental prelude and postlude and an interlude at the end of the A
section of the rondeau. (HAM, No. 68.)

Instruments frequently doubled the voices in the performance of
secular compositions, too. One version of a chanson in a manuscript at
the Escorial in Madrid is provided with the direction *Contra Tenor
Trompette*, indicating that the slide trumpet alone should be used for the
performance of that voice. Although we know that sometimes all voices
of a chanson were performed on instruments, most purely instrumental
performances were those providing music for dancing. One favorite
combination consisted of two shawms and a slide trumpet, another of
harp, lute, and flute. The instruments in the first group were referred
to as *hauts instruments*. This meant that the volume of tone they produced was greater than that of the *bas instruments*, which would include
those in the second group. Thus, the name of the modern oboe is derived
from the French *hautbois*, "a wooden instrument with a large volume
of tone."

SOURCES AND ADDITIONAL READINGS

BessM	FeH	ReMR	ThC
BukS	KeW	SpC	UrC
CaM	MariH	StaM	WagM
	MariM	StrS	

LISTENING ASSIGNMENTS

1. Dufay, Masses: *2000 Years of Music: Gloria ad modum tubae;* P & O, No. 15: Kyrie I from *M. Se le face ay pale.* The tenor of the chanson is in the tenor of the Mass movement. Are the time values of the former followed strictly or freely? (Other Dufay Masses are on the record list.)
2. Dunstable, motets: ParT, No. 18: *Veni Sancte Spiritus,* isorhythmic motet; ARC 3052 or EA 36: *Quam pulchra es* (SteM, p. 19ff). Notice the sound of the passages in 6 technique. EA 36: *Sancta Maria.*
    3
3. Dufay, sacred music: Dec DL 9400: Hymn, *Hostis Herodes;* cantilena, *Vergine bella;* motet, *Ave Regina.*
4. Chansons: Van BG-634: Binchois, *De plus en plus, Filles à marier;* A. de Lantins, *Puisque je voy;* ARC 3052: Dunstable, *O Rosa bella;* EMS 206: Dufay, *Adieu m'amour* (HAM, Nos. 69, 70, 71, and 68).

WRITTEN ASSIGNMENTS

1. Discuss factors influencing conditions in the early Renaissance and circumstances helping the arts to flourish in the fifthteenth century.
2. How much of the *L'Homme armé* tune did Dufay use in the Kyrie I of his Mass by that name? Find the point (how many measures from the end?) in the Agnus III at which the melody begins in reverse and from which it continues in forward motion to the end.
3. Study the music of Binchois' *Adieu m'amour* in P & O No. 16. List the style features discussed in the chapter that you can find in it.
4. Where is the *cantus-firmus* Mass believed to have originated? In what ways do Dufay's Masses show contemporary style changes?
5. What melodies might a composer select on which to base the *cantus firmus* of a Mass? How were the notes usually treated in writing out the *cantus firmus*? Explain the term *verbal canon* and name a composition employing one.

the franco-flemish groups

The fertile valley of commerce in the late fifteenth century was still plowed simultaneously and continuously in opposite directions by a marching cavalcade of merchants; beast and barge that had groaned and creaked northward with tempting luxuries shuttled back around the Alps with merchandise from the north bound for Venice. The law of supply and demand can rearrange the lives of men, who continually throughout the narrative of history have left home and heritage to seek elsewhere a brighter hearth and easier security. Florence had become a leading center for the manufacture of textiles — first wool, then silk — so many a Flemish weaver moved to Florence where he could earn a more prosperous and relaxed existence. From the north came also French and Flemish singers and composers, whose music added beauty and luster to the courts of Italian noblemen.

The invasion of musicians from the north is understandable for at least two reasons. Not only were the northerners better singers, but there was also an element of snobbishness favoring the foreigners over native performers. Musicians were attached to noble families, sheltered, fed, and clothed. Some took the family name; for instance, "Josquin d'Ascanio" thinly disguised Josquin des Prés. But the musicians had only the status of servants. They were not free to leave — the great Brumel was once threatened with prison if he should try to escape his patron's service. Although even the most famous were poorly paid, there were often fringe benefits, such as a good capon now and then. John Hothby, English theorist who was a choir director in Lucca from 1467 to 1486, once received thirty pounds of oil and other gratuities in addition to his salary.

Cambrai was particularly celebrated as a source of good singers. Dufay is known to have sent the best singers from Cambrai to give concerts at the court of Piero de' Medici. This noble family had acquired much of its wealth by acting as protectors of trade routes around Florence. It was just one of many families in Italy that were not only patrons of music but also amateurs in the art. According to Baldessare Castiglione in his *Il Libro del Cortegiano* ("The Book of the Courtier"), to know music was a necessity not only for a gentleman but also for a gentlewoman.

Lorenzo de' Medici (1449-1492), called The Magnificent, one of the most glorious and accomplished of Renaissance princes, wanted to command artists more than soldiers. A lover of painting and architecture as well as music, he supported famous artists, literary men, and musicians such as Michelangelo, Luigi Pulci, and Heinrich Isaac. He owned an impressive variety of instruments. No less interest is reflected in the list made after the death of Cardinal Ippolito, who owned ten bowed string instruments, a cembalo, a large lute, and several wind instruments.

Figure 22. Medici bell (bronze). (Courtesy of the Metropolitan Museum of Art, Crosby Brown Collection of Musical Instruments, 1889.)

Duke Hercules of Ferrara sang and played the gamba; other members
of his family were accomplished on the harp and lute.

OCKEGHEM AND HIS CONTEMPORARIES: THE CHANSON

It may well have been the wealth of the nobility that helped make
possible the copying of beautiful illuminated manuscripts with elaborate
initials and exquisite miniatures. Many are *chansonniers,* devoted to
secular pieces. They have been discovered in libraries in Florence,
Modena, Rome, and other Italian centers of music; others now repose
in the National Library in Paris and a few have come to light in Spain
and Germany. Two important late fifteenth-century sources have found
their way to the United States: the "Mellon Chansonnier" at the Yale
Library, the "Laborde Chansonnier" at the Library of Congress. Most

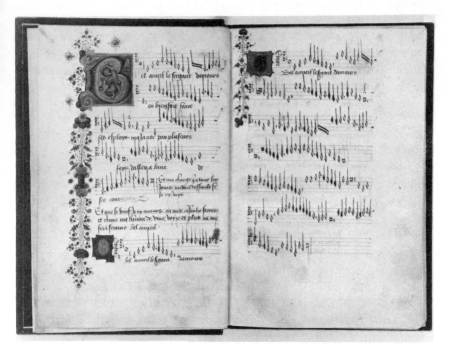

Figure 23. The first two pages of music in the "Mellon Chansonnier," now
at Yale University. The piece is a three-voiced chanson by Busnois called
Bel acueil le sergent. As often happens, the chanson is anonymous in this
source. There is some indication that the manuscript was originally larger;
perhaps the composer's name was lost when the manuscript was trimmed for
binding. (Courtesy of the Yale University Library.)

of these and other sources of the late fifteenth century continued the choirbook format described earlier. Early in the sixteenth century, however, a new arrangement began to take its place: the superius parts of all pieces in a collection were bound in one volume, all alto parts in a separate one and so on — six, seven, or eight part-books were needed for any collection of which the music was in as many voices.

In the generation following that of Dufay the chanson became a favorite among nearly all composers. The men of this generation were born in the years immediately preceding or following 1430, although the exact birth dates of most and the death dates of comparatively few are known with certainty. Our knowledge of the output of fifteenth-century composers is handicapped because in many cases a piece may be attributed to a certain composer in one source and to one or more of his contemporaries elsewhere.

Composers of this generation still favored the three-voiced texture in their chansons, although in sources later in the century a fourth voice has often been added, perhaps by the composer, perhaps by a different hand. It was usually labeled *si placet,* indicating that it was optional. Duple meters began to crowd out the ternary measure still in vogue in the time of Dufay. A piece might begin in ternary measure and change to duple, as, for example, at the beginning of the *b* section of a *bergerette,* a virelai of one stanza only. The rondeau, usually in one of its extended forms, was more than ever the favorite secular form; ballades were composed occasionally; a number of chanson forms were free. In the late fifteenth century the range of music began to extend several steps below the bottom note of the Guidonian hand. This imparted a dark, rich quality to all such passages. The VII$_6$-I cadence began to disappear, displaced in growing proportions by the octave-leap and V-I cadences.

Ockeghem

By far the leading master in this generation was Johannes Ockeghem (c.1420-c.1495), one of the Renaissance composers whose origin was in the Low Countries. He may have been a pupil of Binchois. After a brief engagement as a singer in the choir at the Antwerp cathedral he was one of the court musicians of Charles I at Moulins, but soon after 1450 he was appointed for the rest of his life to the court of King Charles VIII of France. He is one of the composers praised by the renowned contemporary theorist Tinctoris.

Although many of his chansons were famous in their day and beyond, his Masses and motets show him at his best. He has a marked tendency to write in phrases that are not so clear-cut as those of Dufay and his contemporaries. Phrases do not begin and end simultaneously — rather, they overlap, which conveys a feeling of continuity without pauses. The voices seem to flow past most cadences. This is well illustrated in two of his chansons, *Ma maitresse* and *Ma bouche rit*, both virelais. Only at the end of the two sections of each does activity stop completely; elsewhere at least one of the voices is in motion, even through cadences. Imitation occurs rarely in Ockeghem's chansons. In the first of these two secular pieces there is none; in the second there are a few typical examples.

At the beginning of *Ma bouche rit* and of the *b* sections of both pieces there is a stylistic feature associated with many chansons of the late fifteenth century and with the *canzona*, an instrumental piece later derived from the chanson. It is the rhythmic figure ♩ ♪♪│♪ which occurs at the beginning of so many examples that it becomes a cliché. Also present in *Ma bouche rit* is a melodicle 𝄢 ♩♩♩ which we encountered in a slightly different form in Dunstable's *Sancta Maria*. It so overruns the music of the Renaissance that it may indeed be considered "coin of the realm." (HAM, Nos. 74 and 75.)

Busnois and Caron

Both these musical idioms occur in the music of Antoine de Busnes, known as Busnois, a composer most clever and prolific in the creation of polyphonic chansons. Talented as a poet as well, he set to music many of his own texts containing many plays on words, even on his own name and that of his sweetheart. Philippe Caron's chansons were also highly esteemed. His most famous one, *Hélas! que pourra devenir*, preserved in eighteen different sources, is full of ingenious canonic imitation; so is *Vive Charlois*, in all likelihood an instrumental fanfare, perhaps in honor of Charles VIII of France. (AM-E, No. 11[1].)

Polyphonic Masses: Ockeghem

Ockeghem could be most adroit and skillful whenever he wanted to use canon. For his *M. Prolationum* there is no *cantus firmus* — all the movements are canons. The canon Mass seems to have had its origin in the music of the Ockeghem generation; the first example may have been the *M. L'Homme armé* by Faugues. Ockeghem's Mass is a *tour de force* from beginning to end. The piece is *a 4* with the exception of the Pleni and Agnus II, each *a 2* and each still in canon. All four-voiced sections are double canons, although lighter scoring is achieved in the Christe. Between some of the sections in the first four movements the harmonic intervals of the canons increase by one scale degree, from the unison to the octave; for example, the Kyrie I is canon at the unison, the Christe canon at the second, the Kyrie II canon at the third, and so forth. Also, the Kyrie I, Kyrie II, the first half of the Gloria and of the Credo, the Osanna and the Agnus II, are examples of a mensuration canon. In canons of this kind the voices begin simultaneously, but the notes in one voice are longer in mathematical proportion than the corresponding notes in the other — that is, they are in different time values. A canon results in which the time interval among the voices increases continuously as the canon proceeds. A melody to which this technnique is applied need appear only once in the source when provided with different mensural signs. Nearly all sections of this Mass listed above contain double mensuration canons except the two-voiced Agnus, which is a single mensuration canon.

It might appear that music written on such a mechanical principle is aesthetically disappointing in performance. Nothing could be farther from the truth — for this is where Ockeghem's genius is strikingly revealed. Each movement unfolds new beauties to the ear; the sound alone would excite our admiration, especially when we remember the structural plan, which may not be detected by an uninformed auditor. Hearing this Mass is fully as rewarding as listening to any other polyphonic Mass by an outstanding composer. However, it cannot be sufficiently emphasized that no sacred music of the Renaissance, either, is ever fully effective unless heard in the surroundings for which it was composed — a cathedral with its reverberation that cannot be matched in any known way. (P & O, No. 17; ML, V-9.)

Another Mass without *cantus firmus* is Ockeghem's *M. Mi-mi*, so named because of the skip from *mi* in the natural hexachord (e) to *mi* in the soft hexachord (A) in the motive e-A-e-f-e that occurs in the bottom voice at the beginning of each movement. Parts of this Mass lie in quite a low range.

Most of Ockeghem's eleven other Masses are based on pre-existent material. The *M. L'Homme armé* and the *M. Caput* are of the *cantus-firmus* type. The former at the beginning of most movements provides en example of a head-motive: 𝄞 ∎ ⦁ ⦁ ⦁ ∎ or: 𝄞 ∎ ⦁ ⦁ ⦁ ∎ . The Kyrie of this Mass also shows how this borrowed tune with its three-part form ABA is particularly well suited to be the *cantus firmus* of Mass movements naturally divided into three sections, for example, a Kyrie or Agnus. However, as often happens in polyphonic Ordinaries, the tenor is omitted entirely in the Agnus II of this Mass so the second and third parts of the melody occur in the Agnus III. Rather unusual, on the other hand, is the fact that in this Credo and Agnus the tenor much of the time is lower than the bass. The presentation of the tune throughout is straightforward, not paraphrased.

Comparative simplicity of style may be observed in the Christe. Elsewhere rhythmic variety produces a polyphonic web of great flexibility, in a counterpoint of rhythm especially characteristic of the style of this and the next generation. In the scoring of the Agnus III there is also variety in color, provided by several introductory duos involving the middle, upper, and lower voices, before the writing becomes *a 4.* (HAM, No. 73; Omn, p. 28f.)

Ockeghem's *M. De plus en plus,* based on the tenor of Binchois' chanson, is one example of Masses by composers of this generation in which borrowed material is freely treated and seldom appears twice in the same way. At first, the *cantus firmus* may be in its original or nearly original form, perhaps even in long, extended notes; but then the melody is paraphrased in notes whose time values more closely approximate those in other voices, so the texture becomes homogeneous. In the type of polyphonic Ordinary known as the paraphrase Mass, melodic material

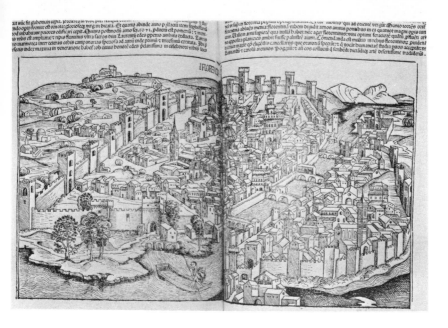

Figure 24. Florence in the fifteenth century. Woodcut from Schedel's **Liber Chronicarum** (1493). (Courtesy of the Nelson Gallery, Atkins Museum (Nelson Fund), Kansas City, Missouri.)

from the *cantus firmus* penetrates the other voices — at least, it is usually extensively paraphrased in the superius. Ockeghem's requiem, the first known polyphonic setting of this text, is a paraphrase Mass.

Polyphonic Masses: Caron

Paraphrase technique characterizes also the Masses of Philippe Caron, which are five in number, several modern works of reference notwithstanding: they are the *M. Accueilly m'a la belle* of which the *cantus firmus* is derived from the tenor of his own chanson; *M. L'Homme armé;* and three whose *cantūs firmi* are based on chant melodies. Of these, the *M. Sanguis sanctorum* was once known only as *M. sine nomine* because its *cantus firmus* went unrecognized for a long time.

Most composers of this generation seem to have been less interested in writing motets. A few by Ockeghem have survived, but they are fully worthy of such a great master; he is said to have written one in thirty-six voices. Only a few motets by Busnois and none by Faugues or Caron have come down to us. Unless further discoveries are made in the future, Ockeghem, Busnois, and their contemporaries will be remembered mainly for their Masses and especially their graceful secular pieces.

Music Printing

The chanson was accorded the honor of being the only kind of music in the first collection of music to appear in print. Ever since the invention of letters in movable type, attempts had been made to discover a satisfactory method for printing music. A commercial process was developed by Ottaviano Petrucci just before the end of the fifteenth century. His first publication (1501) was the *Harmonice Musices Odhecaton* A, containing just under a hundred polyphonic chansons by composers mainly in the generation of Ockeghem and the one following him. Two similar collections by Petrucci were his *Canti B* and *Canti C*, both published in the first lustrum of the new century. Petrucci's process was still rather cumbersome because two impressions were necessary, one for staff lines and one for notes.

THE FROTTOLA

Eleven of Petrucci's collections printed between 1504 and 1514 helped popularize a new type of Italian secular song called the *frottola*. It was cultivated extensively at the court of Mantua, where a dominating personality as well as a particularly interested and alert patron of the arts was Isabella d'Este, daughter of Duke Hercules of Ferrara. The frottola was her special delight and fascination, both in its purely literary form and with music in a new style.

We have been tracing mainly the history of the polyphonic style, organized on the basic of counterpoint, the main underlying principle of art-music since voices began to move in contrary motion. We have

Figure 25. Spinet and case made for Eleanor d'Este, Duchess of Urbino (c. 1540). On the front strip just above the keyboard: "I am rich in gold and rich in sound; do not touch me if you have nothing good to play." (Courtesy of the Metropolitan Museum of Art, Joseph Pulitzer Bequest, Purchase 1953.)

also encountered music that was less contrapuntal, in which voices tended to move together, as in conductus, English $\frac{6}{3}$ technique, and *fauxbourdon*. The frottola was in a very homophonic, chordal style, also called the familiar style. There was only one main melody at the top of its customarily four-voiced structure. There was a strong tendency for all four voices to move in the same rhythm and to begin and end at the same time in clear-cut phrases. Although in these respects its style seems to resemble that of the hymn, the frottola was very gay and nimble, sometimes with many repeated notes in a kind of *parlando* style. Petrucci also published arrangements of frottolas for solo voice and lute, and for lute solo.

The two greatest composers of music for frottolas were Bartolomeo Tromboncino (d. c.1535) and Marco Cara (d. c.1530), both at the court of Isabella d'Este. However, some of the greatest composers of art-music also wrote frottolas; a famous example is *El Grillo* by *Josquin des Prés.* (HAM, No. 95; ParT, Nos. 20, and 21; AM-E, No. 2; AM-N, No. 1.)

JOSQUIN DES PRÉS AND HIS CONTEMPORARIES

If one should attempt to make a list of the greatest composers of all time, Josquin des Prés would have to be the first in chronological order. In sheer ingenuity, talent, and sense of beauty he far outshines all his predecessors and contemporaries.

He was a Frenchman born about 1450. Cardinal Ascanio Sforza of Milan was his patron in 1479. The tendency for composers to be known by the name of their patrons has already been mentioned in connection with Josquin. Subsequently he was a singer in the Papal choir, later

Figure 26. Sculptured marble plaque, portrait (c. 1495) of Lodovico il Moro (1451-1508), a member of the Sforza family, patron of Leonardo da Vinci and other artists. (Courtesy of the Nelson Gallery, Atkins Museum (Nelson Fund), Kansas City, Missouri.)

finding employment with Duke Hercules I of Ferrara and King Louis XII of France. He died in 1521.

The frottola was not the only novelty in the category of secular music. The *formes fixes* began to lose favor in comparison with free forms. Voices increased from the stereotyped three or four of previous generations — five, six, or seven were not uncommon. Imitation, heretofore used with moderation, became a principle of organization and a generating element of form in many works of Josquin and his contemporaries. Usually each text phrase was associated with its own melodic fragment. Both roamed together from one voice to another in contrapuntal over- lapping. Generally, imitation freely pervaded all the voices, a phrase usually being separated by a rest from the one following it. After a rest in any voice, a melodic phrase might initiate a point of imitation; or, it might imitate a phrase already in progress or even just terminated in another voice.

Thus, polyphony was not superseded by the homophony of the frot- tola. Actually, pervading imitation dominated sixteenth-century art- music, but many times we notice the influence of the frottola as a com- poser smoothly merges the two styles. He may allow first one, then the other, to come to the force or he may blend the two in a varied com- bination.

Josquin's Motets

Both styles are illustrated in Josquin's motets. It has been said that, outstanding as he is in everything he undertook, his greatness is most eloquent in this category. It was in his motets that he made his most significant contributions to the style we call Netherlandish, a homogene- ous texture of equally important voices interrelated through extensive use of pervading imitation. Settings in motet style for psalms are rare until the early sixteenth century in the works of Brumel and especially Josquin. Motets in this generation were often much longer than previously, so they were divided into *partes,* or sections, frequently contrasting with each other.

Josquin's *Tu pauperum refugium* ("Thou art the refuge of the poor") is the second half of a motet. It is predominantly in chordal style, al- though some imitative passages occur at the words *errantium* and *veritas;* after the $\frac{2}{2}$ meter begins, imitation is in pairs of voices. Immediately following this passage there is sequential treatment of material in all four voices. Further unification is achieved by the repetition — at the beginning of the $\frac{3}{2}$ passage — of musical material heard at the beginning. Variety in the scoring is provided by pairing voices in high and low registers between passages employing the full four-voiced texture and by the artistic manner in which moments of activity contrast with those of less tension — especially at the end, which gradually relaxes calmly. Two features of the final cadence typify many others in the sixteenth century: the IV-I progression and the absence of the chord third in the final chord. (HAM, No. 90.)

Imitation as a form-producing element is well exemplified in his *Ave Maria . . . benedicta tu*. The motet consists of a very skillful four-voiced paraphrase of a plainsong *Ave Maria*: in all the voices of the motet each text phrase is associated with a paraphrase of its original chant motive. The result is a typical example of pervading imitation, with cadences concealed by overlapping of phrases. (P & O, No. 19.)

Polyphonic and chordal styles are beautifully combined in his *Ave Maria . . . Virgo serena*, also *a 4*. Josquin begins by paraphrasing the melody of this plainsong sequence addressed to the Virgin, after which the polyphony proceeds independently of the model.

tone painting

More composers of the sixteenth century than ever before gave their attention to expressing in their music feelings or ideas present in the texts. We call this tone painting. A very easy, obvious, and even naive way of accomplishing this is to let the melodic line imitate direction up or and down — for example, motion upward when the text says, "He ascended into Heaven," or downward at "He descended into hell," or leap downward when a fall is mentioned. For a setting of the penitential Psalm (130) that begins, "Out of the depths have I cried unto Thee, O Lord" (*De profundis*), Josquin wrote the music in a very low range, employing not the usual clefs but the mezzo-soprano, tenor, baritone, and sub-bass clefs to facilitate the use of an unusually low range without leger lines. In his setting for a portion of Psalm 119, "Remember the word unto Thy servant, upon which Thou has caused me to hope," melodic motives, sometimes very short, are subject to many repetitions one after another, emphasizing the idea of remembering. In connection with this piece we hear through an anecdote that this motet was intended to remind the French king of financial promises that had not been kept.

At the end of *Absalon fili mi* when the text says, "But I shall go down weeping into the grave," the descent is gently depicted as the general level of all the voices sinks very gradually in pitch and the chord roots mostly descend as follows: G Major—E Minor—C Major—A Minor up to F Major—D Minor—B♭ Major up to E♭ Major which then acts as a VI chord in G Minor followed by a V-I in that key. This purely tonal progression is unusual for its time.

Josquin's Chansons

Josquin was extremely adroit in the use of canons, not only in the solemn music of a Mass but also in graceful chansons whose texts are

gay and frivolous. In *Faulte d'argent* there is a two-voiced canon between the contratenor and the *quinta pars*. This is another of Josquin's
pieces in which pervading imitation is the underlying principle of composition. Further unity is gained by much repetition, including a return
of a large part of the beginning, from *Femme qui dort* to the last occurrence of *pour argent se reveille* in the contratenor. (HAM, No. 91.)

Some of Josquin's chansons consist entirely of canons. The light-
hearted *Basiez-moy* exists in two musical settings, one for four voices
and one for six: the former consists of two simultaneous bilinear canons,
the latter of three.

A canon *a 3* is the background of an instrumental fanfare called *Vive
le roi*. This piece illustrates a process both amusing and ingenious. It
consists of deriving musical notes for a *cantus firmus* by means of the
familiar solmization syllables of the hexachord. Josquin derived a series
of pitches as follows, taking advantage of the Latin equivalent v = u:

The melody thus derived forms the fourth voice of the composition. It
is in long notes and is repeated several times, for which the lively three-
voiced canon provides an intriguing foil.

Josquin also used this device to provide the *cantus firmus* for two of
his Masses. He flattered a patron, Duke Hercules of Ferrara, by writing
a Mass whose *cantus firmus* was drawn from the vowels of the duke's
name:

The other instance did not exactly involve flattery. An earlier patron,
perhaps Cardinal Ascanio Sforza, was notoriously stingy. Josquin repeatedly asked to have his meagre salary increased, only to be put off
with an impatient *Lascia fare mi!* ("Leave it to me!"). Finally, Josquin
took the syllables *la sol fa re mi* for the *cantus firmus* of a Mass in which

the promise was repeated over and over in mechanical fashion in the tenor, first in long notes, then more impatiently and insistently.

Josquin's Masses

His Masses cover a wide range of techniques, from the conservative *cantus-firmus* Mass with tenor in long notes and Masses of the paraphrase type, to those written in the parody technique usually associated with the sixteenth century but which, as we saw in Chapter III, occurred in isolated examples much earlier. Petrucci's first book of Masses (1502) was devoted entirely to Josquin's, as were also two more in 1505 and 1514.

Josquin wrote two Masses on the *L'Homme armé* tune. The *M. L'Homme armé super voces musicales* is actually a paraphrase Mass; although the *cantus firmus* is often in long notes, it permeates the other voices consistently. Josquin makes use of the melody forward and backward. In each movement the *cantus firmus* begins one degree higher up the notes of the hexachord (the *voces musicales*) — in the Kyrie it begins on c, in the Gloria on d, in the Credo on e, and so forth — although all movements are still in the Dorian mode. The four-voiced texture is maintained with three exceptions: the Pleni is *a 3;* the Benedictus consists of three two-voiced mensuration canons in succession — the upper voice of each begins in notes twice as long as those of the lower voice; and the Agnus II is a trilinear mensuration canon — one melody is sung simultaneously in three different mensurations. (HAM, No. 89; ML, IV-6 from his *M. L'Homme armé sexti toni.*)

His *M. Ave Maris stella, M. Gaudeamus, M. Da pacem,* and *M. Pange lingua* are paraphrase Masses. For the last named, the plainsong hymn furnishes musical material on which the entire structure is built. Each movement treats the borrowed melody at first rather literally, then paraphrases it with great artistic freedom in all four voices. Although throughout most of the Kyrie, Sanctus and Agnus the style appears quite polyphonic on the printed page, a hearing of the work shows there is actually a smooth blend of chordal style with polyphony. In the two longer movements several purely homophonic passages bring out very clearly certain text phrases, especially *Et incarnatus . . . homo factus est.* (Omn, p. 30ff.)

Josquin wrote other Masses on secular tunes and two canon cycles. He also left us examples of Masses which exemplify stages of development toward the parody Mass and one considered to be the earliest example of a true parody Mass, the *M. Mater Patris.*[2]

Figure 27. "Musical Angels," by Cecchino da Verona (d. 1480). There are many Renaissance paintings of angel concerts, depicting angels singing and playing. Very rarely do we find an instrument poorly drawn, as in this picture of the lute in which the pegbox bends off at a wrong angle. The other instruments are a psaltery, a portative organ, and a harp. (Courtesy of the Nelson Gallery, Atkins Museum (Nelson Fund), Kansas City, Missouri.)

Obrecht: Masses

Conservative tendencies in Mass composition are characteristic of an outstanding contemporary of Josquin, Johannes Obrecht, born in Holland about 1450. Obrecht visited Italy at least once, where he, too, was in the employ of Duke Hercules of Ferrara, but spent most of his life in the Low Countries. His Masses contain his finest work. The *cantus-firmus* principle predominates; one in particular has features of special interest. In the *M. Maria zart*, instead of following the usual procedure of forming the *cantus firmus* by treating the melody as a single unit, he divided it into twelve segments arranged in different series of alternation for each movement. For example, segments 1 and 2 are heard in Kyrie I and Kyrie II (omitted from the more thinly scored Christe), and so on; segments 9, 10, 11 and 12 provide *cantus-firmus* material for the Sanctus. The melody as a whole is not heard until the Agnus I. Progressive tendencies may be found in his *M. Fortuna desperata, M. Je ne demande,* and *M. Rosa plaisant*: each is a parody Mass, the first two using as polyphonic models chansons by Busnois, the last being based on a chanson by Caron. (SteM, p. 71ff.)

Obrecht's Motets

Conservative features typify his motets also; imitation is sometimes rare in their very polyphonic texture. *Parce, Domine* contains only one point of imitation, although it is written in a continuously interweaving, polyphonic style that reminds us of Ockeghem. (P & O, No. 18.) Others, like *O vos omnes,* are more progressive, sometimes full of pervading imitation; in other cases points of imitation alternate with homophonic, chordal passages. (HAM, No. 76b; AM-F, No. 1; SteM, p. 26f.)

Brumel

Antoine Brumel's sixteen polyphonic Ordinaries include a *M. pro defunctis.* This requiem contains a polyphonic setting of the *Dies irae.* For his *M. de beata Virgine* he selected portions of plainsong Ordinaries as *cantus-firmus* material: the Kyrie and Gloria of Mass IX, Credo I, and the Sanctus and Agnus of Mass XVII. Other composers who wrote Masses by this title also turned to these same melodies, sometimes substituting, as did Josquin, the Sanctus and Agnus of Mass IV for those just named.

THE PROPER OF THE MASS

We have seen that polyphonic settings of portions of the Proper were written by members of the medieval Parisian group of composers, beginning in the twelfth century (Leonin's *Magnus Liber* . . .). Interest in this phase of liturgical composition was pushed into the background, however, by the motet in the twelfth and thirteenth centuries. *Organa* of the Parisian school were used in cathedrals as late as the fourteenth century. Although Dufay wrote some settings for the Proper, even these were sung in localities of lesser importance. The first known *Plenariumsmesse* − a complete polyphonic setting of both the Ordinary and the Proper for one liturgical occasion − was by a contemporary of Dufay, Reginald Liebert. Many motets for use in the Proper are preserved in the Trent manuscripts.

Isaac

These motets are the principal forerunners of the *Choralis Constantinus,* the most celebrated composition by Heinrich Isaac (c.1450-1517).

He, too, made Italy his destination, working at first for Lorenzo de' Medici. Before 1500 he entered the service of Emperor Maximilian I, at Vienna, but traveled extensively, spending his last years in Florence. Although he wrote several polyphonic settings of the Ordinary — including the *M. Carminum*, whose *cantus firmus* is based on several German secular songs — he is remembered particularly because of his long work for the cathedral of Constance, begun in 1508 and not quite finished when he died. This awesome undertaking was intended to provide polyphonic settings for the Proper of the Mass for all Sundays and certain special feasts spanning the entire liturgical year. Most settings for the Gradual and Offertory are missing, however. All pieces except Alleluias begin with a plainsong intonation; often the chant melody appears unchanged in one of the voices of the polyphony. (AM-F, No. 2.)

Isaac is represented in Petrucci's *Odhecaton* by five pieces, of which the last three seem to be purely instrumental. One of these, *Hélas que deuera mon cuer*, takes Caron's famous *Hélas! que pourra devenir* as a polyphonic model for a parody. As a composer of purely instrumental music (HAM, No. 88), he may have been preceded by Obrecht, who wrote a number of such works; the latter's famous *Tsaat een meskin* (HAM, No. 78) presents an interesting combination of polyphonic and chordal styles. It is one of the earliest instrumental canzonas, to be discussed in the next chapter. Instrumental works appear also in the *Glogauer Liederbuch*, a collection of chansons, German songs and textless pieces, of about 1460. (HAM, Nos. 82 and 83.)

Sources and Additional Readings

AdI	BukU	FeH	ReMR	ThC
BessM	ColS	HewO	ScheM	ThoC
BriV	CuC	KeW	SpC	UrC
BroA	DrT	LiG	StrS	WagM
		MariM		

Listening Assignments

1. ParT, Nos. 20 and 21: The frottola in its four-voiced vocal form and the lute solo arrangement. Notice (1) the chordal treatment of the text in the former, the main melody being in the top voice; (2) how the continued motion in the lute arrangement helps prevent the evanescent sound of the instrument from actually disappearing.
2. VHMS, Vol. III: Josquin, *El Grillo*. The sound of the cricket is imitated in the rapid *parlando* of this frottola.

3. P & O, No. 19: Josquin, *Ave Maria . . . benedicta.* Observe how the motet is really a four-voiced fantasy on the chant version (p. 63).
4. ARC 3159: Josquin, *Faulte d'argent* and *Basiez-moy.* The canon is completely concealed in the first; the threefold repetition of the second, with varied vocal and instrumental scoring in this recording, brings out the two canons. (Both also on EMS 213.)
5. Dec DL 9410: Josquin, *Fanfare* (*Vive le roi*). An excellent chance to hear the sounds of ancient instruments.
6. *VHMS*, Vol. III: Josquin, Sanctus from *M. L'Homme armé super voces musicales.*

WRITTEN ASSIGNMENTS

1. At what harmonic interval is the double canon in the Sanctus of Ockeghem's *M. Prolationum* (P & O, No. 17 — compare measures 1 and 13)? (Be sure to listen to the recording.)
2. There are clear cadences in the Kyrie of Ockeghem's *M. L'Homme armé* (HAM, No. 73) at the end of each of the three sections and also in the fourth and the seventh bars of Kyrie II. What kinds of cadences are these? Where does a drive to the cadence begin? Where would you say this occurs at the end of Agnus III?
3. What are the mathematical relationships between the notes of the three voices in the triple mensuration canon from Josquin's *M. L'Homme armé* (HAM, No. 89)? Observe how the piece is notated in the original source: it was sufficient to write out the melody only once and place three mensural signs at the beginning:₵3, C, and ₵.
4. Study HAM, No. 146 or preferably Omn, p. 52ff. Explain how the polyphonic model is used as the basis for parody Mass movements.

FOOTNOTES

¹Incorrectly attributed to Jehan Caron in this source.
²For examples showing how parody technique operates see HAM, No. 146 or Omn, p. 52ff.

the golden age
of polyphony

History is like a continually rotating kaleidoscope in which the colored-glass fragments are human traits. These never change, though of course they appear in continually new designs that have an inevitable effect on the countless situations that accompany man's journey. Rare indeed is the traveler who can remember and learn enough from the unavoidable ugly moments to render less disturbing and destructive any similar experience when it arises, as it inevitably will. The struggle for life, wealth, and power is concomitant to our existence; wise almost to the point of non-existence is the man who is content with what he has and is able to realize when one more shove may push his luck too far.

A continual exchange of merchandise between north and south Europe had brought wealth to many communities along the route. But in their efforts to dip more and more from the stream of gold, towns put chains across waterways and began to impose crippling tolls on goods in transit on canals and rivers. The Venetian and Alexandrian monopoly on commerce with the east, causing the prices of luxuries to rise, was a prime factor in the geographical explosion of Europe which had begun with the Portuguese capture of Ceuta in 1419. The Portuguese and Spanish discoveries dropped the curtain on Italian prosperity and caused trade routes to shift from the Mediterranean to the Atlantic. Soon buying and selling with new countries brought the center of world power closer to the western part of Europe. Portuguese and Spanish explorers brought wild dances back from Central America which influenced secular instrumental music until well into the eighteenth century.

SECULAR MUSIC: THE FRENCH CHANSON

Thus, sea power became increasingly important and wars for trade and colonies began to take the place of battles for conquest of European lands. One celebrated battle, led by Francis I of France at Marignan in the middle of September, 1515, was the last great victory of the armored lancer. It was part of a campaign that has been commemorated in a nursery rhyme we learned as children.[1] The Battle of Marignan lives on in a French chanson so famous that it was extensively imitated. The text of *La Guerre*, by Clément Janequin (c.1480-1560), relates the story of the whole encounter, with onomatopoetic sounds. He also wrote other programmatic songs, such as "The Lark," "The Song of the Birds," "The Chattering of Women" and "The Cries of Paris." Numerous shorter compositions, such as the charming "This Month of May," contributed more to his fame. His chansons incorporated tendencies we met in the Italian frottola: light, fast, strong rhythm; homophonic, chordal style with main melody in the top voice; syllabic settings of texts; four-voiced texture; short, clear-cut phrases.

Claudin de Sermisy (c.1490-1562) was another important composer of chansons with these features. The influence of the Netherlandish style in the early sixteenth-century French chanson is noticeable in compositions by Thomas Crécquillon (d. c.1557) and Jacques Clément (c.1510-1556), better known as Clemens non Papa. Their chansons are more contrapuntal, with fuller texture, smoother melodic lines, and a less marked rhythmic beat. (HAM, No. 107; Omn, p. 35; P-&O, No. 20; AM-N, Nos. 2 and 3.)

The first collection of music printed in France contained French chansons in the styles just described. It was the work of Pierre Attaignant, who used movable type from the workshop of Pierre Haultin, consisting of many small pieces combining notes and segments of staff lines – a single-impression method used even in recent years.

Music in the familiar, chordal style characterized also the Spanish *villancico* of the late fifteenth and sixteenth centuries. It showed formal traits (*ABBA*) derived from the virelai. (HAM, Nos. 97 and 98; ParT, No. 19; AM-N, No. 4.)

The Italian Madrigal

About 1530 the first examples of the new Italian madrigal began to appear. This was the result of a number of influences, but principally it was a fusion between a more serious type of frottola with the Netherla dish contrapuntal style. The Italian sixteenth-century madrigal became

Figure 28. "The Allegory of Music: The Muse Euterpe" by Laurent de la Hire. The muse is tuning a chitarrone, one of the archlutes. On the table is a lute, also a violin showing the old form of neck and fingerboard, and recorders. (Courtesy of the Metropolitan Museum of Art, Charles B. Curtis Fund, Purchase 1950.)

one of the most popular and widely cultivated forms in the history of music.

There were not many features the old fourteenth-century madrigal had in common with the new, two of the main ones being the name and subject matter. Whereas the former was strophic and ended in a ritornello, the main traits of the latter could be summed up as follows: (1) it was in very free form; (2) the poetry selected for the musical setting was of the best quality — Petrarch was the favorite source; (3) the earliest madrigals were *a 4* and very chordal; whenever polyphony occurred it was very simple. Later ones tended to combine polyphonic and familiar styles in a homogeneous texture consisting of five or more voices, all of which were equal in importance; the text might be treated in melismatic or syllabic style.

Tone painting, or word painting, was thrust into prominence by the proliferation of the sixteenth-century Italian madrigal and remained a favorite device of composers for two centuries. Madrigalists seized upon every possible opportunity to underline natural sounds, bodily movements, emotions, and ideas by means of devices that became clichés. They depicted cruelty or bitterness, disappointment in love, and the like by means of a sudden dissonance frequently involving an unexpected chromaticism; or, they represented grief by means of a chromatic melodic line, which usually, though not always, descended.

the first publication

The earliest composers were mostly Netherlanders, although Italians then took up the category and successfully helped bring the form to its peak. Philippe Verdelot (c.1480-1540), either a Frenchman or a Walloon, and the Italian Costanzo Festa (c. 1480-1545) were represented in the first known printed collection of madrigals: *Madrigali de diversi musici libro primo* (1530), published by Antonio Dorico. (HAM, No. 129; AM-E, No. 5.)

Madrigals of the chordal type were also written by Jacques Arcadelt (c.1504-1567), a Netherlander working in Florence whose famed *Il bianco e dolce cigno* ("The White, Sweet Swan") found echoes in a work by the Englishman Orlando Gibbons which centered around the swan song. (HAM, No. 130; Omn, p. 36; AM-E, No. 6; ML, IV-11.)

Adrian Willaert (c.1485-1562), another Netherlander, choirmaster at St. Mark's cathedral in Venice from 1527, became one of the most influential musical personalities of the century. His madrigals composed in the early 1530s are predominantly chordal, but those written after 1540 show the encroachment of Netherlandish traits.

later madrigalists

Two of Willaert's students were the Italian Nicolo Vincentino (1511-72) and the Netherlander Cipriano de Rore (1516-65). The former tried to apply intricacies of Greek theory to his madrigals, with the result that they contain very unusual chromaticisms, and degree inflections involving large and small semitones. Rore, too, was influenced by chromaticism, but less for its own sake and much more for the purpose of expressing effectively the meaning of the text.

The five-voiced texture of Rore's *Da le belle contrade* ("From the beautiful countries") combines intricate polyphony with familiar style — contrapuntal passages alternate with more chordal writing. Sighs at parting are illustrated in the music at the phrase, *T'en vai, haimé!* ("Thou art going, alas!"); immediately thereafter, "Thou leavest me alone" (*Sola mi lasci*) is sung by a single voice. The music portrays the cruelty of love with an A major chord (on the word *dolente*) followed abruptly by one on C minor (*Ahi crud' amor*); the idea of "repeating" (*Iterando*) is naively underlined where that word occurs. (HAM, No. 131; AM-E, No. 7.)

Orlando di Lasso, also known as Roland de Lassus (c.1532-94), another native of the Low Countries, was one of the most celebrated composers of the century. Extremely cosmopolitan, he successfully wrote all kinds of contemporary vocal music, but was at his best in shorter forms. His secular compositions include not only Italian madrigals but also French chansons and songs with German texts having a decidedly popular flavor. (HAM, No. 145.)

The Italian Luca Marenzio (1553-99) brought the madrigal to a high point of artistic perfection. His inspired imagination was nearly limitless in its variety, so that the most delicate shades of meaning in the text were tastefully enhanced by the music. An unexpected minor chord in the second measure of *S'io parto, i' moro* ("If I leave, I die") suggests the "death" of parting. The meter of the poetry is matched by very flexible rhythmic groupings in the music which by no means keeps a rigid pulse; thus, important words are brought out naturally ("and yet I still must leave thee"). In *Madonna mia gentil* the idea of standing on earth (*Stando in terra*) is twice represented by a cessation of motion in the music, while the word *paradise* is insistently supported by ascending melodic lines. (HAM, No. 155; P & O, No. 27; AM-E, No. 10.)

Whereas Marenzio treated chromaticism with great moderation, Carlo Gesualdo, Prince of Venosa (1560-1613) went to extremes in degree inflection and abrupt progressions for the sake of tone painting. Many of his passages can hardly be said to involve modulations — often they are boldly arbitrary tonal leaps. For this reason his madrigals are extremely difficult to sing, a fact readily evident in many a modern recording. On the other hand there are places suggesting passages by Wagner, as, for example, at the opening of *Moro lasso*. At the beginning of *Io pur respiro* there is a sudden rest after the first syllable of *respiro* ("I breathe"), as though to imitate this action. The word *anguish* (*dolore*) is repeatedly associated with a chromatic line, and at the last occurrence of this word a D major harmony, over a pedal point on g, goes by chromatic motion to a minor chord of the seventh on g; *pitiless* (*dispietato*) is illustrated by a harmonic leap from F major to F-sharp major; at the next *Alas!* (*Ahi*) the harmony jumps from C-sharp major to A minor. (HAM, No. 161; Omn, p. 37ff; ParT, No. 33; ML, IV-13.)

monteverdi

In tracing the history of any discipline it is only natural that we are interested mainly in those figures who have achieved excellence. There are occasionally exceptions who tower above even those who are merely excellent. Such a person was Claudio Monteverdi (1567-1643), straddling two eras, with one foot in the Renaissance and the other well into the Baroque.

Monteverdi's first secular works were in *Canzonette a tre voci,* published in Venice in 1584. The *canzonetta* was a type of popular native song, a light, vocal piece often containing the stereotyped rhythmic pattern ♩ ♩ ♫♩ ♩ ♩ ♩ familiar to us in the English ballett (cf. p. 140). Having found in the canzonetta a style he felt was well suited to his purposes, he published books of five-voiced madrigals in rapid succession: Book I, 1587; Book II, 1590; Book III, 1592. (ML, IV-12.)

By the time Book IV was published (1603) the new opera had begun its long, triumphant road. For some time Italians had been rebelling against the Netherlandish invasion with its highly complicated, contrapuntal style that made the text hard to understand. They called this "laceration of the poetry," and said a piece of vocal polyphony was like a palace in which people were walking about independently on different floors. Basing their principles on ideas they found in Plato and in Greek tragedy, they maintained that the text was more important than the music; above all else, the text must be understood.

The madrigals in Monteverdi's Book IV became the subject of a dispute initiated by Giovanni Artusi, a conservative who objected to modern features in Monteverdi's compositions, such as his uninhibited manner of handling dissonances, many of which were unprepared. Monteverdi's reply to Artusi's attack was in a very brief message "To My Learned Readers," at the beginning of Book V of his madrigals (1605), in which he said harmony and all musical problems are an outgrowth of the poetry and the text must be the master, not the servant of the music. In his madrigals the words dominate the music, which faithfully reflects, with free and expressive harmonies, ideas presented in the words. Monteverdi saw the main melody, the soloistic element, as a counterplay to the bass, as though there were polarity between them or as though they were rivals. Within this lies the beginning of the *stile concertante*, the contrasting style, a dominating factor in the style of the new Baroque.

The musical texture of Monteverdi's madrigals may vary from polyphony to chordal recitation. The latter provides a subtle and delicate beginning for *Ecco mormorar l'onde* ("Hear the murmuring of the wave"); it furnishes dramatic moments that alternate with more lyric ones in *Sfogava con le stelle* ("Under the stars of the nocturnal sky.") At the beginning of *Ohimé, se tanto amate* ("Alas! if you love so much") vivid text illustration represents the sighs. The mournful feeling is heightened by unprepared dissonances as the two upper voices make their double entry. Monteverdi has great fondness for a Picardy third in the top voice at a cadence (*morire, sentire*). In spite of frequent answering back and forth and imitative entries among the voices, the style is predominantly homophonic. Chordal recitation plus animated repetition of short fragments of text and music near the end illustrate, first, many sighs in succession, then, the "thousands of alases." (HAM, No. 188.)

Monteverdi continued to write madrigals all his life, but those of the last four books are true Baroque compositions. He prolonged the

Figure 29. This is a corner consisting of two flat walls, but they are done in very intricate wood inlay designed with the purpose of deceiving the eye. It is a corner of a room, from the fifteenth-century palace of the Duke of Urbino at Gubbio, which may now be seen in its entirety at the Metropolitan Museum in New York. The wood inlay depicts a lute, two cornetts, and a vielle, as though inside an actually nonexistent cupboard. A portative organ is represented as on the "bench" (part of the wall). (Courtesy of the Metropolitan Museum of Art, Rogers Fund, 1939.)

life of the madrigal by transforming it from a Renaissance composition to one embodying ideals of the new era.

SACRED MUSIC

Highly imitative, Netherlandish style dominated the music of Nicholas Gombert (c.1480-1556). He is best known for his sacred polyphony, having written ten Masses, 169 motets, and eight magnificats that have been preserved. Two of his ten Masses employ *cantus-firmus* technique; the other eight are parody Masses. In accordance with a growing custom he often added another voice to the usual five or six for at least one section of the Agnus. His pervading imitation is smooth and artistic and his fondness for asymmetry made his polyphony very flexible. The rhythm of each line is very free and independent, with almost continual activity and motion, few rests, and rarely any pure homophony. His motet *Super flumina* illustrates a craftsmanlike and beautiful treatment of imitative style, with artistic building of vocal lines. Contrapuntal motion in overlapping phrases carries through most of the cadences so the music comes to rest in comparatively few places. The style represents a neat balance between polyphony and homophony, pervading imitation and chordal passages, all with a highly sensitive feeling for appealing modality. Sometimes points of imitation treat two subjects simultaneously. Toward the end, interest is heightened by rhythmic changes. (HAM, No. 114.)

Clemens non Papa and Adrian Willaert, both mentioned previously, are two other significant composers of sacred music in the generation between Josquin and Palestrina. We have fifteen Masses by Clemens, all but one of the parody type. Their style is less consistently imitative than that of Gombert; homophonic passages are more frequent and of longer duration. He, too, usually increases the number of voices in the final movement. One mark of his style is a fondness for wide upward leaps, at least partially filled in as the voice moves back downward degreewise. This may be seen in his motet *Vox in Rama* in which descending scale lines after upward leaps of fifths, sixths, and octaves effectively represent the ululation of Rachel mourning the loss of her children. The work is highly imitative but not with complete consistency. Of particular interest is the Neapolitan sixth a few measures before the middle of the piece. One quality of sixteenth-century music most intriguing to our ears is it modality — that is, formations based on the ecclesiastical modes. However, as we move forward in time we notice an increasing tendency toward major and minor modes. The occurrence of the Neapolitan sixth is one indication of this. (HAM, No. 125.)

Vox in Rama does not make use of the plainsong melody associated with it in the *Liber usualis,* but the *cantus-firmus* motet is exemplified by Willaert's six-voiced *Victimae paschali laudes* in which the first two lines of the Easter sequence appear first in the *sextus;* then the *quintus* presents the melody in its entirety. The texture is rich almost to the point of being lush. The presence of many leaps of a fourth and fifth in the bass is another indication of growing feeling for functional harmony. (HAM, No. 113; AM-F, No. 7.)

The old *cantus-firmus* principle continues in one of the two *L'Homme armé* Masses by Christóbal de Morales (c.1500-1553), the first important Spanish composer of the sixteenth century. Two-thirds of his

Figure 30. "Allegorical Representation of Instruments" by Jan Brueghel, part of a much larger painting. Left: part of a two-manual harpsichord, a drum, and bass trombone; on the floor, left foreground: a rebec and lute, with a family of recorders in their case; behind and above: a chest of viols; under the three-legged stool: a cornett; on the floor to its right: a shawm and lira da braccio; under and back of the three-legged stool at right: a recorder, a shawm (or straight cornett?), a tenor-alto viol, a large S-shaped cornett, and another viol. Part-books are on the music stands and on the floor. (Courtesy of The Bettman Archive.)

twenty-one remaining Masses are based on plainsong melodies or motets. Two of the former are *Missae de beata Virgine,* one *a 4* and the
other *a 5.* Strong Netherlandish style characteristics the first, in which
the plainsong melodies usually associated with Marian Masses furnish
material for a paraphrase Mass. Paraphrase technique and pervading
imitation also characterize his *Magnificat octavi toni;* different polyphonic settings for each of the even-numbered verses, sung by soloists,
alternate with choral performances of the odd-numbered ones. Melodies
of the plainsong are paraphrased throughout the polyphony. (ParT, No.
23.) Pervading imitation with overlapping phrases distinguishes his
motet *Emendemus in melius* ("Let us make amends"), based on a
Roman responsory for Ash Wednesday which is heard successively in
four voices as the motet opens. Soon a fifth voice, the Contralto II, intro-
duces a new melody with a different text, the words said by the priest
as he distributes the ashes: "Remember, man, that thou art dust, and
unto dust thou shalt return." (HAM, No. 128; ParT, No. 23; AM-F,
No. 6; *M. de beata Virgine* pr. WagM, p. 457ff.)

The Protestant Reformation

Occasionally a rising flood of new ideas runs into a larger main-
stream of complacent tranquillity. The resulting turbulence may change
the direction of the original quiet flow and cause ebullience by reason
of its own inherent dynamism. An entirely new stream of musical activity
poured from the confluence with Protestant reform.

Martin Luther (1483-1546) was born about the time Josquin des
Prés was reaching manhood. His words of respect for this famous composer have been often quoted. Originally he did not want to break away
from the Catholic church but to reform it. Among other things, he
favored more participation in the Mass by the congregation, who, not
understanding Latin, would just "stand with their mouths open" as
Luther put it. Although he did not propose the complete elimination
of Latin from the service, he did want more use of the vernacular. He
preferred the retention of the Latin Kyrie and Gloria — the term
Lutheran Mass refers to one consisting of these two movements only.
This is also known as a *Missa brevis,* but it should be made clear that
this term may also mean an Ordinary of all five movements composed
as compactly as possible, often favoring homophonic over polyphonic
style in order to shorten the time needed for the service.

For each of the Latin Credo, Sanctus and Agnus, Luther wanted to
substitute a chorale, a hymn tune with a German text. German chorales
are available for use in place of any portion of the Latin Mass. Luther

Example 17.   Hassler: Mein G'müt ist mir verwirret.

a.

My   soul   is   full   of   tor - ment,   I

love   a   maid - en   fair

b.

O   Sa - cred   Head,   now   wound - ed,   With

grief   and   shame   weighed   down

himself wrote many chorale texts, such as *Ein' feste Burg ist unser Gott*
("A Mighty Fortress Is Our God") and in many cases adapted existing
melodies, some of them even well-known love songs, to set his words
to music. Isaac's *Innsbruck, ich muss dich lassen* ("Innsbruck, I now must
leave thee") became *O Welt, ich muss dich lassen* ("O world, I now
must leave thee"). This practice continued for a long time; one of the
best-known chorales is *O Haupt voll Blut und Wunden* ("O Sacred
Head, Now Wounded"), the tune taken from a love song by Hans Leo
Hassler (1564-1612) shown in Example 17. Some tunes, of course, were
newly composed. The original rhythm of the melody often represented
the meter of the text more sensitively than later versions, with their
steady march of notes in stately, uniform values.

For more than two centuries these simple tunes inspired composers
of art-music to write a variety of derivative forms which became the
backbone of Protestant church music. Polyphonic versions of the chorales
began to make their appearance early in the 1520s and continued to be
published at frequent intervals. Settings varied from simple ones *a 4*
in chordal style to versions drawing on *cantus-firmus* principles; some
were imitative polyphonic motets. At first the melody was in the tenor.
The simple forms were for the congregation in church and at home, the

others for performance by a trained choir. (HAM, Nos. 108 and 111; ParT, No. 24.)

The Calvinists were much less tolerant of art-music than the Lutherans and banned church organs, which they even took out and destroyed. Objecting much more to the retention of Latin and the Catholic liturgy, they believed the only music acceptable for worship to be settings of rhymed, metric versions of the Psalms, many of which were composed by Louis Bourgeois (b. 1510), Claude Goudimel (1514-1572), and Claude Le Jeune (1528-c.1600). The tune to the Doxology now sung in Protestant churches came from a more metrical version which appeared originally in a Calvinistic Psalter. (HAM, Nos. 126 and 132; ParT, Nos. 25 and 26.)

The Counter Reformation

The separation of the Lutherans and the Calvinists from the Catholic church was the result of serious ecclesiastical difficulties that had long been recognized. It was largely through the efforts of Emperor Charles V that the much-postponed meeting of a council began in 1545 at Trent. Its three main goals were the settlement of doctrinal disputes, a crusade against heathens, and, of greatest concern to us, the reform of undesirable abuses in administration, appointments, duties of the clergy and so forth. In the nearly twenty years over which the various sessions were spread the Missal and Breviary were revised; also, there was clarification regarding what constituted music acceptable for use in the liturgy. Contemporary practices to which objections were raised included the use of music that had vulgar associations or that obscured the words. Two members of the council proposed limiting the music to plainsong only, but further study overcame this threat to polyphony. Music performed at sessions of the council — notably Jacobus Kerle's *Preces speciales* — and other pieces examined by its members convinced them that polyphony was acceptable if the words were not obscured, if the counterpoint and the rhythm were not too complicated, and if the harmonies were not too distracting. Thus, the minds of the listeners would not be diverted from divine subjects.

palestrina

When considered by members of the council, the music of Giovanni Pierluigi da Palestrina (c.1526-1594) was thought to possess musical qualities they believed were ideal. His style consists of a balanced blend of homophonic features with those of Netherlandish polyphony. Motion within any one voice is predominantly stepwise. When melodic skips of more than a third occur, the line usually turns back to fill in at least part of the gap with degreewise motion in the opposite direction. Leaps of more than a fifth are rare and the total range of any one voice almost never exceeds a ninth. If occasionally two skips in the same direction follow one another, the larger precedes the smaller when the motion is upward, vice versa when it is downward. Excess chromaticism is avoided. Dissonances are carefully approached and resolved. The total result is a style that is pure, unemotional, objective, and impersonal — ideally reflective of the spirit of plainsong itself. Palestrina meticulously observes the correct accentuation of each word. For these reasons the Palestrina style was considered the most perfect for sacred music even after the Renaissance, when styles changed radically. Students today who take courses in modal or sixteenth-century counterpoint follow rules evolved from analytic observation of Palestrina's style.

Born in the town of Palestrina, Giovanni Pierluigi studied music in Rome. Although his genius as a composer was repeatedly rewarded by a succession of positions in Roman chapels, his personal life was clouded by tragedy when two of his sons, his brother, and his wife all died within the space of a few years. He soon married again, however, the lady having been the widow of a furrier whose business she had inherited. Thus, for the last fourteen years of his life Palestrina was a fur dealer while at the same time a productive composer of primarily sacred works.

Although he wrote more than 80 madrigals, these are far outweighed in number and importance by his 105 Masses, 450 motets, and other liturgical pieces. The Masses represent all the types we have encountered: 8 *cantus-firmus* Masses, 34 of the paraphrase type, 52 parody Masses, 5 canon Masses, and 6 free Masses.

His most famous one is the *M. Papae Marcelli*. For a long time it was believed this piece was composed by Palestrina in order to impress those cardinals appointed to consider the problem of plainsong vs. polyphony at the Council of Trent. Actually, the Mass was written before their meeting.

In the first Agnus Dei of this Mass, which is *a 6*, degreewise motion predominates; the upward leap of a fourth, present in all voices in the imitative opening, is filled in by subsequent degreewise motion downward. If one or more skips occur in succession, either their directions are reversed or, if in the same direction, they form a triad in root position. Skips of a fifth are rare; there are only two leaps of a sixth and these are minor. Leaps of an octave occur freely — there was no objection to these because they were considered to be nearly the same as note repetition. Also, octave leaps help the voices cross without restriction so the melodic lines may be as logically vocal and as beautifully shaped as possible. Correct declamation of the text is carefully observed. Thus it is evident how the preceding principles are borne out by observation of the music itself. (HAM, No. 140.)

The rise and fall of plainsong melodies may well have been affected by the accents of the individual words (cf. p. 23). The shape of Palestrina's melodic lines was also influenced by word accents, but the overall musical form of the lines received at least equal consideration and at times took precedence. His four-voiced motet *Sicut cervus* has been cited as one containing especially beautiful arch-shaped lines, whose ascent and descent are balanced in striking symmetry. Sometimes the accented syllable of a word coincides with a melodic peak, but by no means always — thus, it is evident that the shape of the musical line is also an important factor. This composition provides an especially fine example of the pure, impersonal, elegant quality of Palestrina's counterpoint. There is almost no degree inflection; all voices are equally important; each line is as beautifully shaped as any other; the vertical aspect is as masterfully handled as the horizontal. His style comes as close as possible to approximating in polyphony the spiritual quality of plainsong. (HAM, No. 141.)

Until comparatively recent years any mention of Renaissance music to the musical public automatically brought with it the thought of Palestrina as almost the sole representative. However, people are now coming to realize he was not the unique phenomenon he was once thought to be. He is still just as bright a star, but we now know more about the rest of the constellation in which he was so brilliant. (Omn, p. 52ff; P & O, No. 24; AM-F, No. 8; SteM, p. 65ff; ML, IV-4, 7.)

lasso

Many details that characterize melodic lines as woven by Palestrina are also present in a typical fabric of sacred music by Orlando di Lasso. In various ways he was as illustrious as his contemporary; however, Palestrina served the church all his life, while Lasso's main patron was the court at Munich. Although the latter's more cosmopolitan existence did not require him to emphasize sacred music, it is in his motets that we find his greatest achievements. Like Palestrina, Lasso gave very careful attention to the setting of the text. Whereas Palestrina seldom allowed the cool, controlled objectivity of his music to be affected by emotions contained in words of the text, Lasso often used tone painting. Thus, his music is more intense, more red blooded, more colorful and vivid. Rhythms are more irregular; leaps are more frequent (although there is still a high percentage of degreewise motion); degree inflection and modulation are introduced with greater freedom; mood changes are more sudden. All this is done with the best of taste, artistry, and craftsmanship. He has a strong feeling for tonal progressions of chords: his bass lines tend to move in fourths and fifths, Palestrina's more degreewise. Lasso's lines are less melismatic, less conjunct, than Palestrina's. He is vigorous and robust while Palestrina is refined and fastidious.

In Lasso's setting for the first verse of the third penitential Psalm the rhythm of the music often duplicates that of the individual words. Degree inflections soon appear, leading to modulation. Modality and a tendency to functional harmony are combined. The latter may be noticed in the motion of the bass line, which is quite angular, with many wide leaps. A sudden change of mood takes place at *neque in ira tua* as the text refers to God's anger. The Picardy third in the final cadence contrasts with Palestrina's general preference for a bare chord without any third at many cadences. The setting for the twentieth verse of the same

Figure 31. "The Musicians" by Michelangelo Caravaggio. Lute, violin, cornett, and part-books. (Courtesy of the Metropolitan Museum of Art, Rogers Fund, 1952.)

Psalm is typical in its very polyphonic, imitative opening followed by a gradual but insistent change to homophonic style. This artistic miniature typifies Lasso's fondness for a structural outline in which a quiet, relaxed opening builds up very gradually to a high point of intensity which, soon before the end, yields to a gentle resumption of slower motion that closes the piece as tranquilly as it began. (HAM, No. 144.)

The Introit from his polyphonic Requiem incorporates the plainsong, with very few changes, in the tenor; other voices frequently paraphrase the chant. Successive wide leaps at the second occurrence of *aeternam* in the top voice would have been quite foreign to Palestrina. Everywhere his careful regard for the text setting is evident; accented syllables get longer time values, very frequently even notes higher in pitch, than those given to unaccented ones. (HAM, No. 143.)

Although Lasso wrote 53 Masses, they do not show him at his best. Most of them are parody Masses. His *M. Puisque j'ai perdu* embodies many of his characteristics, such as beauty of melodic line, careful treatment of text, reflection of emotion in the music (especially the *Osanna*), balance of activity among the parts, imitation at close time intervals, and beautiful and effective handling of duos (*Domine Deus*). (Omn, p. 47ff; P & O, No. 23; AM-F, No. 11; SteM, p. 55f.)

Both Palestrina and Lasso were very prolific: Palestrina's 105 Masses overshadowed Lasso's 53, but the former wrote only 450 motets in comparison with the latter's 1200. Altogether the total of Lasso's compositions is close to two thousand.

victoria

A third great composer of sacred polyphony in the late sixteenth century was the Spaniard Tomás Luis de Victoria (1548-1611). His name often appears in the Italian spelling, Vittoria. Before he was twenty he studied in Rome, where Palestrina may have been his teacher. He soon became a priest, a fact which was reflected in his dedication to sacred music only. Although he wrote no madrigals his sacred style is characterized by a type of tone painting that is madrigalesque, more obvious and naive than the subtle text treatment of Lasso. Of his twenty Masses, eleven parody his own motets: his *M. O magnum mysterium*, based on one of his two best-known motets, shows a marked tendency to homophonic style. The original motet on which the Mass is based opens with a plainsong formula very reminiscent of the example cited on page 30 as one of those associated with the Dorian mode. The polyphonic opening of the other famous motet, *O vos omnes,* soon dissolves into chordal style that dominates the whole work in spite of occasional independence of voices. Homophony is emphasized in passages where chords are repeated to heighten the dramatic effect. Degree inflection is used in a way that produces a feeling of D minor rather than the Dorian mode. Rhythms are flexible in spite of the homophonic reiteration. (HAM, No. 149; AM-F, No. 9; SteM, p. 57ff, p. 61ff; ML, IV-2, 8, 9.)

The Venetian School

Rome, Munich — and now Venice, for this was destined to become one of the most influential centers in music history. When refugees came from mainland cities in 452 A.D. they found a group of fishermen's huts scattered near the islands of a lagoon. The move of the people to the archipelago did not take place until there was danger of an attack by Pepin in the eighth century; this settlement of the islands themselves marked the beginning of Venice.

The present church of St. Mark's is the third on the site. When Moslems destroyed the burial place of that saint in Alexandria, a wooden building to protect the relics was erected in Venice in 828. This burned in 976 and the structure replacing it was extensively remodeled in 1063 with the help of Byzantine and Lombard workmen. It is extremely rich in material and decoration, partly because by law every merchant who traded in the east was required to bring back some material adornment to add to its treasure. Venice, known as "the jewel of the sea," was a center of hedonistic pomp and ceremony in the sixteenth century. The services at St. Mark's mirrored the glory of the state and were resplendent with ornate, elaborate processions and ritual pageantry.

The church was arranged so that there were two choirs as well as two organs, one on either side. This physical distribution of its musical forces gave special stimulus to music for divided choirs. The idea was not a new one — divided choirs had long since been used to underline the parallel structure of Psalm verses and to vary the presentation of plainsong. However, literature for this disposition of musicians received special attention in the hands of choirmasters and organists at St. Mark's. (ParT, No. 28.)

willaert

Adrian Willaert was one of the first among choirmasters to gain renown and one of the first in a long line of law students to abandon this career for music. After studying in Paris he went to the court of Count Alfonso I (d'Este) at Ferrara, then to the chapel of Archbishop Ippolito II (d'Este) in Milan. He was at St. Mark's from 1527 until his death. Through his students, Willaert's influence was far-reaching and he may be said to have founded a Venetian school of composers. The full, rich texture of Venetian music is well represented by his motet, *Victimae paschali laudes*, already discussed.

g. gabrieli

One of the famous organists at St. Mark's was Andrea Gabrieli (1510-86), who may have been a pupil of Willaert. His nephew, Giovanni Gabrieli (1557-1613), brought the "colossal Baroque" closer in the size of musical forces he employed — as many as six choruses impressively augmented by large groups of many kinds of instruments. These were assigned independent passages of their own, thus forming instrumental choirs that added to the dazzling effect of the performance. Although it is actually too early to use the term, his *In ecclesiis* is really a cantata, with a variety of musical groups — solos, choruses, brass and string instrumental choirs — taking part in a composition that is sectional. There are many textures: contrapuntal, chordal, soloistic, polychoral — and the piece even forecasts the thoroughbass of the next century, for only the bass line of the organ part is given. It is a truly Baroque composition. (HAM, No. 157.)

More famous by far is Giovanni's *Sonata pian' e forte* of 1587, the first known composition to assign certain instruments to certain instrumental voices and to provide indications for loud and soft. It is also one of the first to use the term *sonata*. This piece, too, is polychoral: one choir consists of cornett and three trombones, the other of viola and three trombones. These two groups play alternately, then together, throughout the work. (HAM, No. 173; Omn, p. 63ff.)

INSTRUMENTS AND INSTRUMENTAL MUSIC

The lute reached a peak of popularity in Italy in the sixteenth century. It was an instrument on which polyphonic music could be played; it was handy to carry and blended well with instruments of any other kind; it was good for solos or accompaniments; it was not too expensive. A standard form had five pairs or courses of strings plus a single one, tuned G c f a d' g'. Larger sizes were called archlutes.

The first printed instrumental volumes of music were in four collections of lute music published by Petrucci in 1507 and 1508, each volume called *Intabulatura de lauto*. The title refers to the fact that lute music is not really notation but a tablature, a sort of diagram showing where the fingers are to be placed on the strings. Francesco Spinaccino made the arrangements in the first two books; original compositions in Book IV were by Joanambrosio Dalza. Literature for the lute included pieces for voice and lute; transcriptions of vocal pieces for lute solo; and ricercars, fantasies, and dances.

The earliest sixteenth-century instrumental ricercars were simple, short, nonimitative preludes and postludes such as those an organist might play in improvising freely for a few moments. Dalza even wrote a prelude to a ricercar, calling it *Tastar de corde con li soi ricercar dietro* ("An improvisation on the strings with its own ricercar following"). Soon the ricercar became polyphonic and imitative, thus turning into an instrumental counterpart of the motet. But the fantasia became nearly synonymous with the ricercar, so by the late sixteenth century both fantasy and ricercar meant an independent instrumental piece, usually imitative. (HAM, Nos. 99 and 121; ML, IV-14.)

Dances

In the second half of the fifteenth century dances became separated into court and folk dances. Printed manuals of instruction began to appear.

Figure 32. Lute by Giovanni Hieber, sixteenth century. (Courtesy of the Instrument Museum, Brussels.)

Between 1450 and 1550 the *basse danse* flourished. It was slow and stately with gliding movements, *branles* (pron. brawls, meaning side-steps), and bows. Music was provided by quite a variety of instruments — in addition to the more customary two shawms and slide trumpet, the lute, harp, drum, cornett, trombone, and flute played in various combinations.

Dances were in pairs, the music for the second, more lively dance being often a variation of the first, a slower one. The combination of a *pavane* and *galliard* found great favor in the sixteenth century. The former was a peacock dance, proud, dignified, showy, and solemn, while the latter was full of thrusts and leaps. About 1530 the number of gay, lively dances increased; in addition to the galliard there was the *canaries;* the branle, which became a chain choral dance; and the *courante,* originally a pantomimic wooing dance, which by the end of the seventeenth century had become slow. This same kind of metamorphosis applied to two important dances brought back from the New World by explorers: the *saraband* and *chaconne,* introduced in the late sixteenth century, were at first very wild and shocking, but soon after 1600 became quite tame. (HAM, Nos. 137 and 154; Omn, p. 41ff; P & O, No. 22.)

The Canzona

Instruments continued to be used during the performance of vocal polyphony. By 1550 published collections often included on the title page some phrase such as "To be sung or played" — any of its melodic lines could be performed either vocally or on an instrument.

Fully as important as the growth of dance music was the development of a new category in music literature. The light, gay French chansons of Janequin and his contemporaries were so popular in Italy that many were reprinted for purely instrumental ensembles under the name *canzona francese.* Then composers wrote entirely new pieces published under the title *canzona alla francese,* or *canzona da sonar.* The characteristic rhythmic cliché on a repeated note at the beginning of many a chanson (♩ ♩ ♩ ♩♩) characterized also its instrumental counterpart, the canzona. Soon imitative ricercars were written for instrumental ensembles and keyboard instruments. The ricercar was the main forerunner of the fugue; from the ensemble canzona developed the Baroque *sonata da chiesa.* (HAM, Nos. 88, 115, 118, 136; P & O, No. 21.) The theme and variations appeared well before 1550, especially in Spanish music for the vihuela, the instrument which, though shaped like a guitar, was the Spanish equivalent of the lute. (HAM, Nos. 122, 124 and 134.)

Renaissance ensembles often consisted of groups of instruments of the same kind in different sizes. At first, ensemble music was not written for any specific instrumentation — it might have been played on any family of wind or string instruments. In England, the terms *consort* or *chest* were used to refer to a family of instruments.

Wind Instruments

By 1600 recorders were made in nine sizes. More raucous reed instruments, such as the krummhorn or cromorne, the rankett, and the shawm, also came in a full assortment of sizes. The trumpet was an exception to the vogue for instruments in complete families. Trumpeters began to specialize in playing the instrument in one of several ranges: the most skillful players, aided by a shallow mouthpiece, could produce the highest partials, called the clarin register, where diatonic and even chromatic passages are possible; other players specialized in lower ranges.

String Instruments

There were two main families of bowed string instruments. The *viola da braccio,* or arm viol supported on the shoulder, was the principal ancestor of the modern violin family. The violin had achieved its present form by about 1525; it did not become popular, however, until after the beginning of the seventeenth century.

Most favored in the Renaissance was the other main string family, that of the *viola da gamba,* or leg viol, in as many as six sizes. All of these were held with the pegbox upright and the lower bout resting on or between the knees. The gamba, or viol, had a flat back, very sloping shoulders, and thinner strings, usually six in number, tuned like the lute in fourths with a third in the middle; the strings of the treble sounded d g c′ e′ a′ d″. The alto-tenor and treble sizes were thicker than the viola and violin. The bow was held with the palm of the hand up, the stick — which had a convex, not a concave curve — lying across the inside surfaces of the fingers.

A less important family was the *lira da braccio,* used in Italy during the Renaissance. It may have been a descendant of the vielle or fidel. Like the latter, it had vertical pegs; two off-the-fingerboard strings were drones. One tuning given for it is much like that of the violin, which seems to have inherited some of its physical characteristics.

The Organ

Organs increased in size and range. Pedal keyboards were in use by the fifteenth century, but for a long time they were a great rarity in

Figure 33. Members of gamba and violin families, for comparison of size, shape, and stringing. Left to right: bass gamba, cello, tenor-alto gamba, viola, treble gamba, violin, treble gamba. (Photo made by the author.)

certain localities, even in London in Händel's time. Early in the fifteenth century we begin to find pieces intended as substitutions for portions of the Mass. The first complete organ Mass is considered to be that of Girolamo Cavazzoni in his *Intavolatura* of 1543. (HAM, No. 117; ParT, No. 15.)

the toccata

Keyboard instruments had their own category of music called the *toccata*, referring to the striking or touching of the keys. The first toccatas contained only rapid, showy scale passages and full chords combined in a rhapsodic, free style and form. Soon, however, free passages were balanced by stricter sections in imitative style, the form of the whole then depending on alternation of brilliant, pseudo-improvisatory sections with others showing influence of the imitative ricercar. (HAM, No. 153; ParT, No. 29.)

The Clavichord and Harpsichord

Stringed keyboard instruments included the clavichord, in which each string sounds when struck by the tip of a flat piece of metal called a tangent. Placed at the far end of each key it rises to strike the string as the key is depressed. In the harpsichord each string is plucked by a

Figure 34. Italian **lira da braccio.** (Courtesy of the Instrument Museum, Brussels.)

Figure 35. Inlaid gamba including a view of the city of Paris, by Gaspar Duiffoprugcar (1514-1571), a celebrated maker. (Courtesy of the Instrument Museum, Brussels.)

sharp point called a plectrum, fastened on a hinge to an upright piece of wood called a jack that rests on the far end of each key. In old instruments the plectrum was a quill; in modern ones it is usually made of hard leather or plastic. When the key is depressed, the jack rises and the plectrum actuates the string, the hinge permitting the plectrum to slide back past the string without sounding it as the jack drops into place. The spinet and virginal are in the harpsichord family because their strings are made to sound in the same way. In a harpsichord the strings extend directly away from the player at right angles to the keyboard; in a spinet, they extend diagonally away from the keyboard; the strings of the virginal are in a line parallel to the keyboard. It was

Figure 36. Modern harpsichord. (Courtesy of Frank Hubbard.)

Figure 37. Flemish virginal, about 1568, bearing the arms of the Duke
of Cleves. (Courtesy of the Victoria and Albert Museum, Crown Copyright.)

once thought this instrument was named after Elizabeth I, the Virgin Queen of England — but the term existed before she was born. Cembalo, a shortened form of clavicembalo, is another name for the harpsichord. This term refers to the application of keys (*claves*) to a cymbalon, a type of dulcimer. The harpsichord was known by the beginning of the fifteenth century, but the earliest preserved specimen, in the Victoria and Albert Museum, dates from 1521.

ENGLISH MUSIC IN THE SIXTEENTH CENTURY

Music that English composers wrote for the harpsichord beginning late in the sixteenth century occupies a favorite and cherished place in the literature of the instrument. But among English music earlier in the Renaissance were works of singular beauty deserving to be known better than they are.

The half century after the death of Dunstable was a comparatively low point in musical creativity in Britain. There are no famous names, but research is bringing to light more music written in this period than was previously believed to exist. Some fifteenth-century songs show evidence of having been based on dance tunes; others, like "Tappster, drinker, fill another ale" may have originated with minstrels. Many songs of this century were carols for Easter as well as Christmas. (HAM, No. 85.)

Sacred Music

English music of the early sixteenth century was rather conservative in style when compared with contemporary accomplishments in continental music; counterpoint contained only a few points of imitation, although the music of John Taverner (c.1495-1545) includes canon and other devices showing the influence of Ockeghem and Josquin.

Taverner was the first in a distinguished group of English composers — although his annual salary as master of the children in Cardinal Wolsey's College was ten pounds plus room and board and other gratuities, amounting in all to perhaps fifteen pounds. Of his eight Masses, two are of special importance. His *Western Wynde Mass* was the first English polyphonic Ordinary based on a secular tune. It consists of thirty-six variations on the melody, placed in the superius. It is full of style contrasts: homophonic passages *a 4* alternate with melismatic, polyphonic duos. In his *M. Gloria tibi Trinitas* was discovered the source of the *cantus firmus* for a large group of instrumental pieces called *In*

nomine written by English composers from Taverner to Henry Purcell.
(HAM, No. 112; SteM, p. 30ff, p. 33ff.)

tallis

Thomas Tallis (c.1505-85) was called to the chapel of Henry VIII
about 1537. His finest work is in his motets and lamentations. He, too,
abandoned the earlier, less complicated style to adopt the pervading
imitation of his contemporaries on the continent. A *Mass for Four Voices*
is quite chordal, however; it is unified by a head motive and harmonic
progression that occur at the beginning of each movement. By far his
most famous composition is his forty-voiced motet, *Spem in alium nun-
quam habui,* for eight five-voiced choirs. These sing antiphonally in
various combinations most of the time, but all forty voices join in three
climaxes and in the final seventeen measures. The piece may have been
written for the fortieth birthday of Queen Mary. (HAM, No. 127; SteM,
p. 45ff.)

The New Anglican Service

During the lifetime of Tallis a momentous event changed the course
of music history in England: the reformation of public worship. Conditions in sacred music were completely changed — new forms were
demanded; new texts in the vernacular required a new kind of musical
expression; new methods had to be invented. The course of a natural
development had been cut off as though by the axe of the king's execu-
tioner, and all that English composers had done in sacred music to that
point was no longer of any use. Tallis' *Dorian Service* was one attempt
to produce a satisfactory substitute for the old liturgy.

In the new liturgy the *Service,* consisting of the unchanging parts
of Morning and Evening Prayer, or the *Short Service,* chordal and syllabic, were substituted for the Latin Mass. The place of the motet was
taken by either the *full anthem,* for chorus throughout, or, later, the
verse anthem, for one or more solo voices with organ or string instruments alternating with choral sections. (ParT, No. 27.)

byrd

William Byrd (c.1543-1623) was supposedly "bred up to Musick
under Thomas Tallis." He always remained a Catholic, so it is not surprising he wrote three Latin Masses, one each for three, four, and five
voices. At the opening of his Latin motet, *Non vos relinquam,* he treats
two points of imitation simultaneously — a point in the two upper voices
occurs together with a different one (Alleluia) in the lower two; then
each motive is treated similarly in the opposite pair of voices. The

Alleluia motive unifies the whole work. His "Christ Rising Again" is a verse anthem. The upward direction of the musical phrase at the beginning line of text is only one of many examples of tone painting scattered liberally throughout his works. (HAM, Nos. 150 and 151; Omn, p. 39f; P & O, No. 25; AM-F, No. 13.)

tomkins

Thomas Tomkins (1572-1656) was another of the outstanding composers of sacred music. His full anthem, the tender and poignant setting of "When David Saw that Absalom Was Slain," is a high point in artistry, in which the many repetitions forcefully underline David's frustration and distraught grief. (HAM, No. 169.)

gibbons

Orlando Gibbons (c.1583-1625) had honorary degrees bestowed on him by both Oxford and Cambridge. Most of his important compositions are dated after 1600. He contributed substantially to the repertory of Anglican sacred music; his verse anthem, "This Is the Record of John," is especially well known. (HAM, Nos. 171 and 172; Omn, p. 45f.)

Instrumental Music

Gibbons was rated by his contemporaries as one of the best organists and virginalists of his time. He left some very beautiful music for the virginal, a favorite pair of pieces being "Pavana the Lord of Salisbury" and "Galiardo." These were in *Parthenia or the Maydenhead of the first musicke that ever was printed for the Virginalls* of 1612 which included also pieces by John Bull (c.1562-1628) and William Byrd. (HAM, No. 178 and 179; ParT, No. 30.)

The repertory for the virginal contained a wide variety of forms: transcriptions of vocal pieces, dances, variations, and fantasies. These included many examples of the *In nomine*, instrumental fantasies on the melody by Taverner. Pieces by this name were also written for consorts of viols. (HAM, No. 176; ParT, No. 36; ML, IV-15, 16.)

My Ladye Neville's Booke is a manuscript collection of forty-two pieces by Byrd; *The Fitzwilliam Virginal Book* is another manuscript with 300 compositions by different men. Another printed collection, for virginal and viol, was called *Parthenia In-Violata* (about 1614). Other outstanding virginalists were Giles Farnaby (c. 1560-1620) and Thomas Morley (1557-c.1603) who was also famous for his treatise, *A Plaine and Easie Introduction to Practicall Musicke* (1597). (Omn, p. 41ff; P & O, No. 29.)

The English Madrigal

Morley was an important composer of madrigals as well. Although some secular part-songs had been written throughout the sixteenth century, the madrigal did not flare into brilliance in England until nearly sixty years after it began to arise in Italy. A collection of Italian madrigals with English words, called *Musica Transalpina,* published by Nicholas Yonge in London in 1588, precipitated an intense interest in the madrigal among British composers. The musical style of the prototype was continued by the English. There was much tone painting; chromaticism was one means to this end, but it was employed with restraint and good taste. An offshoot of the Italian *balletto* was the English ballett,[2] characterized, like its model, by "fa-la-la" refrains and strophic form. (HAM, Nos. 158, 159, and 170.)

Many English madrigals are gay love songs, but others overflow with plaintive, wistful sadness. In England, as in Italy, the madrigal was a form of vocal chamber music with only a few performers taking part. When the host would bring out the madrigal books, it was a spice that enlivened many a social occasion. In many cases these were printed so that when the music, with all voices printed on one page or on one spread, was laid flat on a table each member of the small group of singers sitting around it found his text and notes facing him.

In 1601 Morley published a collection in honor of Elizabeth I called *The Triumphs of Oriana* — modeled, again, on a similar Italian publication. To this book leading composers of the day each contributed a madrigal, twenty-five in all, dedicated to the Queen. Thomas Weelkes (1575-1623) and John Wilbye (1574-1638) were two other madrigal composers of renown, and there were many others who added to the voluminous literature. (Omn, p. 45f; P & O, No. 28; AM-E, Nos. 16 and 17.)

the ayre

Some of the most expressive and artistic of the madrigals, called *ayres,* were written for solo voice with lute accompaniment. The list of English lutanist song writers is also extensive, but most gifted was John Dowland (1562-1626). His "Flow, My Tears," known also as "Lachrymae," touched many hearts with its simple, plaintive sincerity. The familiar way in which it was mentioned by dramatists of the period — Thomas Middleton, Ben Jonson, John Fletcher, Philip Messinger — proves it must have been intimately known to theater audiences for many years. The beginning of its melancholy, unpretentious melody is the little formula we encountered much earlier in the literature of the era: 🎼. This incipit of Dowland's song was imitated in other Elizabethan pieces. (HAM, Nos. 162 and 163; ParT, No. 34; AM-E, No. 20; AM-N, Nos. 5 and 6.)

The small space we can give to the English virginalists and madrigalists is all out of proportion to the refreshing charm and appeal of their music. Too often, the music of England has been abruptly dismissed as peripheral, but her sons have shown they can produce harmonies that are of a particularly distinctive individuality, in which that famous sense of sonority weaves combinations of invigorating, rare, and sometimes austere beauty.

> If music and sweet poetry agree,
> As they must needs (the sister and the brother)
> Then must the love be great, twixt thee and me,
> Because thou lov'st the one, and I the other.

> Dowland to thee is dear; whose heavenly touch
> Upon the lute, doth ravish human sense:
> Spenser to me; whose deep concert is such,
> As passing all conceit, needs no defence.

> Thou lov'st to hear the sweet melodious sound,
> That Phoebus' lute (the queen of music) makes:
> And I deep delight am chiefly drowned,
> When as himself to singing he betakes.

> One God is God of both (as poets feign)
> One knight loves both, and both in thee remain.[3]

SOURCES AND ADDITIONAL READINGS

BeK	BukU	DonI	FelEM	MarD
BesA	BusL	DonO	FuV	ReMR
BessM	CoJ	EinM	HubT	SaH
BlC	CoT	FeH	HuS	SchrMC
BlR	CuC	FelEC	JeC	UrC
BraI	DarP		JeP	WagM

LISTENING ASSIGNMENTS

1. P & O, No. 20: Créquillon, *Chanson*. Notice the rhythmic cliché at the opening. The keyboard arrangement is full of figurations so the small sound of clavichord or harpsichord may not die away.

2. ParT, No. 33: Gesualdo, *Moro lasso*. The motion quickens when the text speaks of giving life (*dar vita*). Chromaticism underlines the thought of dying (*moro, morte*) and the words *alas!* (*Ahi*) and *painful lot* (*dolorosa forte*).

3. Dec DL 9409: Morales, Kyrie and Agnus from *M. de beata Virgine*. If WagM is available, follow the music and observe how the plainsong permeates the polyphony.

4. VHMS, Vol. IV: Palestrina, Sanctus from *M. Aeterna Christi munera* and Agnus II from *M. brevis*. Notice how the plainsong material is used in these movements. Pervading imitation is at varying time intervals. Observe the canon in the second example. Listen to his *M. Papae Marcelli* (ARC 3182).

5. P & O, No. 23: Lasso, *Tristis est anima mea*. A beautiful example of pervading imitation. Two motives are imitated at the beginning. Motion in the voices is evenly distributed and takes turns among them. There is a drive to the cadence at the end.

6. VHMS, Vol. IV: Victoria, *O Domine Jesu*. In this motet the voices enter one after the other but the imitation does not continue through all of them. From the fourth measure on, the style is predominantly homophonic.

7. ParT, No. 28: Hassler, *Laudate Dominum*, polychoral motet. The two choirs alternate antiphonally, emphasizing the structure of the Psalm verses.

8. VHMS, Vol. IV: G. Gabrieli, *In ecclesiis* (HAM, No. 157). Notice the tremendous variety of all kinds in this magnificent piece.

9. P & O, No. 22: Lute dances. An example of a pair of dances, slow and fast, the second being musically derived from the first.

10. ParT, No. 27: Tallis, "Hear the Voice and Prayer of Thy Servaunts." How would you describe the style of this piece?

11. P & O, No. 25: Byrd, *Ego sum panis vivis*. How does the style compare with that of a Josquin motet?

12. ParT, No. 36: Gibbons, *In nomine*. The *cantus firmus* from the Taverner Mass may clearly be noticed.

13. ARC 3053: Gibbons, "The Silver Swan" (Omn, p. 45ff). What styles do you observe in this madrigal?

14. EA–34: Dowland, "Flow, My Tears." There is marvellous suppleness in this musical setting. Listen also to ParT, No. 34.

WRITTEN ASSIGNMENTS

1. How would you characterize the style of Janequin's *A ce ioly moys* in Omn, p. 35? What does it have in common with *L'Alouette* ("The Lark") in HAM, No. 107?

2. What style dominates Arcadelt's *Voi ve n'andat' al cielo* in HAM, No. 130? In what ways is variety introduced?

3. Compare the two settings of the German chorale in HAM, No. 111, or of the Calvinist Psalm in ParT, Nos. 25 and 26. Which version(s) would be better suited for a trained choir? Why? How do these more elaborate settings (and the piece in ParT, No. 24) resemble the style of pervading imitation?

4. Select any melodic line of the Agnus I from Palestrina's *M. Veni sponsa Christi* (P & O, No. 24). In what ways does its motion conform with principles set forth in the text? Is there a high or low percentage of degreewise motion? How much degree inflection is there? What is the melodic range?

5. What is the musical relationship between the fast saltarello and the more stately opening of the passamezzo in HAM, No. 154a?

6. Compare the styles of the various sections of the canzona in P & O, No. 26. What cliché is present? What musical influences do you notice in this piece?

7. Discuss the structure of the toccata in HAM, No. 153. Show how the piece is formed in sections that contrast with one another.

8. What is the difference between the action of the clavichord and the harpsichord?

9. Study the Tallis Responsorium in HAM, No. 127. Of what very old polyphonic technique does it remind you? In what way is the polyphony very representative of its time?

FOOTNOTES

[1]"The king of France, with forty thousand men, Marched up the hill and then marched down again."

[2]The archaic spelling serves to distinguish this form from the ballet.

[3]Richard Barnfield, "Sonnet I," *Poems in Divers Humors,* London, 1598.

appendix

The following are intended to provide representative suggestions, not a complete list. The sequence of the text has been followed as closely as possible, but some overlapping was unavoidable. In many cases, when pieces mentioned in the text are included on a record, this fact is mentioned. A second number in parentheses is that of the stereo version. Label abbreviations are in accordance with the Schwann catalogue. MHS (Musical Heritage Society) is by subscription only.

Composer, Title or Other Classification	Record Number
Primitive: pounding songs, dance songs, rattles, drums	Folk FE 4201
———— Singing with instruments	Folk FE 4402
———— Vedic chanting	Folk FE 4431
———— Work songs; instruments	Folk FE 4427
———— *Man's Early Musical Instruments*	Folk FE 4525
———— Songs; musical bow	Folk FE 4477
———— Songs; slit drum; musical bow; flute	Folk FE 4483
———— UNESCO Collection: A Musical Anthology of the Orient (sixteen records)	Musicaphon BM 30 L 2001-2016
2000 Years of Music: Greek, Jewish, Gregorian music; *Congaudeant Catholici*; troubadours and minnesingers; *Gloria ad modum tubae* (Dufay); Josquin; German choral music; Palestrina; Lasso; madrigals; harpsichord and clavichord music; dances	Folk FT 3700
Records belonging with P & O (music to c. 1600)	Haydn 9038/40
Records belonging with ParT (music to c. 1600)	Haydn HSE 9100/2

Victor History of Music in Sound (*VHMS*), Vol. I: Greek and Jewish music	Vic LM-6057
VHMS, Vol. II: Mozarabic, Ambrosian, Gregorian Chant; Liturgical Drama (*Quem quaeritis*); Secular Monody; Parallel Organum; Early Polyphony; *Congaudeant Catholici;* Summer Canon; Medieval Dances; Medieval English and French Polyphony	Vic LM-6015
Gregorian Chant: First Mass of Christmas	ARC 3142(73142)
——————— Third Mass of Christmas	ARC 3143(73143)
——————— Second Vespers and Compline of Christmas	ARC 3102
——————— Mass for Easter Sunday	ARC 3090
——————— Easter Liturgy	Cap 35116
——————— Requiem Mass and Burial Service	ARC 3031
——————— Requiem Mass	Soc. Fr. 174.049
——————— Mass of St. Benoit, Mass of St. Cecilia	Soc. Fr. 174.066
Examples of Plainsong	London LLA 14
Chants of the Church (including the four Marian antiphons)	Vic LM-2786 (LSC-2786)
Ambrosian Chants	Vox DL 343
Play of Daniel	Dec DL 9402(79402)
Play of Herod	Dec DX 187 (DXSA 7187)
Carmina Burana	Tel (s)AWT 9455
Troubadour and Trouvère Songs	EA-12, MHS 675
Adam de la Halle: *Jeu de Robin et Marion, rondeaux;* Dances of the thirteenth and fourteenth centuries	ARC 3002
German Songs (Walther von der Vogelweide, Isaac)	West XWN 18848
Music of the Twelfth and Thirteenth Centuries (Parisian School, Motets, Troubadours and Trouvères, Minnesingers, Estampie)	EMS 201
Cantigas de Santa Maria	EA-23, MHS 677
Early Music of England, Flanders, Germany, and Spain (Estampie)	Tel (S)AWT 9432-C
History of Italian Music: Gregorian and Ambrosian Chant, *Ars nova*, Frottola, Lute and other instrumental music, Palestrina, Marenzio, Monteverdi et al.	Vic ML-40000
Spanish Medieval Music: *Cantigas*, Liturgy of Santiago de Compostela, *M. de beata Virgine*	Dec DL 9416(79416)
Leonin and Perotin	EA-21, MHS 676
Leonin and Perotin; chansons and motets of the thirteenth century	ARC 3051

French *Ars antiqua;* conductus and motets   EA-35
VHMS, Vol. III: French Polyphony (including   Vic LM-6016
    Ma fin est mon commencement and
    Kyrie from Machaut Mass); Italian
    Madrigal, Ballata; English 6 tech-
                                    3
    nique, part-songs, and church music
    of the fifteenth century; Dunstable;
    Dufay; Binchois (*Filles à marier*);
    Ockeghem; Obrecht; Josquin (*El
    Grillo,* part of *M. L'Homme armé*);
    Taverner (part of *M. Gloria tibi Trini-
    tas*); instrumental music (Isaac)
Machaut: Mass; Perotin: *Viderunt, Sederunt*   Van BG-622
Machaut: Mass and Ten Secular Works   ARC 3032
Madrigals and Dances from the Squarcialupi   ARC 3003
    Codex; Dufay; Five Sacred Songs
    (*Vergine bella, Flos florum, Alma
    Redemptoris Mater*)
Spotlight on Strings (demonstrations of lyre,   Vox DL 320
    dulcimer, psaltery, lute, harp, gamba,
    rebec)
Spotlight on Winds (demonstrations of bull   Vox DL 312
    roarer, bamboo flute, pan pipes, re-
    corders, shawm, krummhorn, old
    oboe)
Spotlight on Keyboard (demonstrations of harp-   Vox DL 362
    sichord, virginal, early organ, hurdy-
    gurdy)
Songs and Instrumental Pieces of the Fifteenth   ARC 3222(73222)
    Century (recorders, fiddles, psaltery,
    cornett, krummhorn, large lutes,
    hurdy-gurdy)
Medieval and Renaissance Instruments   Turn TV 4019
                                                     (340195)
Spanish Songs of the Renaissance (good pictures   Angel 35888
    of instruments in accompanying folder
    — as well as beautiful singing!)
English Medieval Songs (St. Godric Songs, early   EA-29
    love lyrics, "Worldes blisce": mono-
    phonic)
English Polyphony of the Thirteenth and Early   EA-24, MHS 678
    Fourteenth Centuries ("Worldes blisce-
    Domino": polyphonic)
Fourteenth and Early Fifteenth-century English   EA-31
    Polyphony (Side 2 all from Old Hall)
Medieval English Carols and Italian Dances   Dec DL 9418(79418)
English Medieval Christmas Music ("Alleluia   Count 521
    psallat and Gloria": HAM No. 57;

Dunstable: "Sancta Maria": HAM No. 62)	
Dunstable: Sacred and Secular Music (*Sancta Maria, Quam pulchra es*)	EA-36
Music of the Medieval Court and Countryside (Leonin; Ductia and Estampie; Dufay: *Vergine bella*)	Dec DL 9400
Dufay: *M. L'Homme armé*	Lyr LL150
—————— *M. Se le face ay pale;* Obrecht: *M. Sub tuum praesidium*	Van BG-653
—————— Lasso	Tel TM 1 (TMS 1)
—————— Mass passages, motets, hymns	Tel (S)AWT 9439
—————— Chansons (*Adieu, m'amour, Ce jour de l'an*)	EMS 206
Masterpieces of the Early French and Italian Renaissance	None H-1010(71010)
Dufay, Binchois, Busnoys, et al.: vocal and instrumental	None H 1058(71058)
Arnold de Lantins: *Puis que je voys;* Dufay: Hosanna from *M. Se le face ay pale;* Binchois: *De plus en plus, Filles à marier*	Van BG-634
Music of the Renaissance	Lyr LL86
Ockeghem: *Ma bouche rit, Ma maitresse,* etc.; Dunstable: *O Rosa bella, Quam pulchra es*	ARC 3052
—————— *M. Prolationum, Requiem*	Musicaphon MB 464(964)
—————— *M. Ma maitresse, M. mi-mi*	Musicaphon MB 409(909)
—————— *M. mi-mi, M. Fors seulement*	Lyr LL108
Josquin (*El Grillo*), Cara, Arcadelt, et al.	Lyr LL75
Motets: Dufay, Lasso, Josquin (*Ave Maria . . . Virgo serena*), Victoria (*O vos omnes*)	Per SPL-597
Josquin: *Faulte d'argent, Baisiez-moy,* etc.	EMS 213. ARC 3159(73159)
—————— "Fanfare" (*Vive le roy*), *M. Pange lingua*	Dec DL 9410
—————— *Vive le roy;* Brumel, et al.	None H 1012 (71012)
—————— *M. Hercules dux Ferrarie;* Ockeghem: Motets	Mus. Guild M-7
—————— *M. Pange lingua;* Le Jeune: Six polyphonic chansons	MHS 617
—————— *M. de beata Virgine*	Vox DL 600
Isaac: "Innsbruck"; Brumel, Josquin, Festa, Obrecht	ARC 3223(73223)
—————— Vocal and instrumental pieces; Obrecht: *M. Fortuna desperata*	Dec DL 9413(79413)

—————— "Innsbruck," etc. Beautiful gamba ensemble .... Cantate 91 107

—————— Motets from *Choralis Constantinus* .... Count 546

—————— *M. Carminum*, "Innsbruck," *Jubilate* from *Choralis Constantinus* .... West XWN 18633

Spanish Music of the Fifteenth and Sixteenth Centuries .... Musicaphon MB 431(931)

VHMS, Vol. IV: Italian Madrigals (Marenzio); English Madrigals (Wilbye, Weelkes, Morley); French chansons (Costeley, Sermisy); Victoria (motet); Palestrina (Mass movements); Lasso (motet and 2 sections from *M. Puisque j'ai perdu*); English sacred music (Tallis, Byrd, Morley, Gibbons); Lutheran church music; G. Gabrieli (*In ecclesiis*); Lute songs, instrumental ensembles, keyboard music .... Vic LM-6029

Janequin: *Ce moys de Mai, Song of the Birds;* Le Jeune, Josquin, Lasso .... Dec DL 9629

—————— *L'Alouette, La Guerre, Song of the Birds* .... Musicaphon MB 428(928)

—————— *La Guerre, Ce moys de Mai;* Monteverdi: *Sfogava con le stelle* .... Van BG-604

Le Jeune: Chansons .... None H 1001(71001)

Arcadelt, Cara, Landini, Rore, et al. Voice with lute .... West XWN 18776

Arcadelt: *Il bianco e dolce cigno* .... Van BG-639

—————— *Il bianco e dolce cigno;* Isaac: "Innsbruck;" Dowland, Lasso .... Vic CAL-904 (CAS-904)

Songs and dances by Attaignant, Crécquillon, Gombert, Clemens non Papa, Lasso, Sermisy, et al. .... Per SPL 738

Marenzio: six madrigals; Gesualdo: six madrigals (including *Moro lasso*) .... ARC 3073

Gesualdo: *Moro lasso;* Monteverdi: Canzonettas .... Musicaphon BM 17 E 011

Monteverdi: Madrigals from the Fourth Book (including *Sfogava con le stelle*) .... Haydn HSL 141, 142

—————— Madrigals (including *Hor ch'el ciel e la terra, Ecco mormorar l'onde*) .... Angel COLH 20

Court and Ceremonial Music of the Early Sixteenth Century (Josquin, Compère) .... None H 1012(71012)

Gombert: *M. Je suis desheritée;* Crécquillon: motets .... None H 1051(71051)

Clemens non Papa: Psalm settings .... Cantate 11 16 KS

Spanish composers: Morales, Victoria, et al. ... None H 1016(71016)

Spanish Music of the Renaissance (Milan: *Pavana;* Morales: Kyrie and Agnus from *M. de beata Virgine*) .... Dec 9409(79409)

Mein G'müt ist mir verwirret and two versions of the melody as a chorale	GC C R 4008
Psalms by Goudimel and Le Jeune	Musicaphon EK 110
Psalms by Louis Bourgeois	Musicaphon EK 111
Palestrina: *Sicut cervus, Stabat Mater,* etc.	Angel 35667
Palestrina: *M. Papae Marcelli*	ARC 3182(73182)
———— *M. sine nomine, M. Ecce ego Joannes*	(S)OL 269
———— *M. Aeterna Christi munera*	Argo RG 186 (2RG 5186)
———— *M. Iste confessor, M. sine nomine*	Lyr LL49
———— *M. Hodie Christus natus est, Improperia*	ARC 3243
———— Josquin, Lasso, Attaignant, Bull, Byrd	Lyr LL109
Lasso: Motets	MHS 624
———— *Requiem,* motets	Lyr LL87
———— *M. Vinum bonum,* motets	Lyr LL113
———— *Seven Penetential Psalms*	ARC 3134/5 (73134/5)
———— *M. Puisque j'ai perdu,* motets	ARC 3077
———— *St. Matthew Passion*	Vox DL 400
———— German, French, Italian songs	ARC 3076
———— Morley, Josquin (*"El Grillo"*)	Vic LM-7043 (LSC 7043)
Victoria: *M. O magnum mysterium, M. O quam gloriosum*	Lyr LL46
———— Motets (including *O magnum mysterium*)	Musicaphon MB 441(941)
———— *O magnum mysterium;* Lasso; Monteverdi: *Sfogava con le stelle*	None H 1026(71026)
———— *M. quarti toni,* motets (including *O vos omnes*)	MHS 612, Music Guild M-41
G. Gabrieli, Hassler, Palestrina, Victoria, Lasso	MHS 634
———— Motets	Vox PL 8830
———— Venetian Polychoral Music	Tel (S)AWT 9456
The Gabrielis and their contemporaries (ricercars, canzonas, *Sonata pian' e forte*)	ARC 3154(73154)
G. Gabrieli: *Sacrae symphoniae, Canzoni, Sonata pian' e forte*	Van BG-611
Renaissance Band (demonstrations of instruments)	Dec DL 9424(79424)
Instrumental Music from the Courts of Queen Elizabeth and King James (recorder, flute, shawm, krummhorn, cornett, gamba, sackbut, portative, harpsichord, percussion)	Dec DL 9415(79415)
Canzonas and Dances (cornett, sackbut, shawm, recorder, gamba, portative, regal, harpsichord, percussion)	Dec DL 9419(79419)
English Lute Music	Vic LD 2560
French Dances of the Renaissance	None H 1036(71036)

Eight Centuries of Music for Recorders	Kapp 9049
Byrd: Music for Voice and Viols (*In nomine,* etc.)	EA-37
Taverner: *Western Wind Mass,* motets	Argo RG 316 (ZRG 5316)
Tallis: *In jejunio et fletu, Lamentations of Jeremiah, Mass for Four Voices*	Dec DL 9404 (79404)
Music of the Liturgy in English (Gregorian, Anglican)	Col ML 4528
Easter Matins in King's College Chapel, Cambridge	Argo RG 120
Byrd: Three- and Four-part Masses	Lon 5795
―――― Four- and Five-part Masses	EMS 234
―――― Latin motets	West XWN 18402
―――― Great Service	Van VRS 453
Gibbons: Anthems, Madrigals and Fantasies ("This is the Record of John," "Silver Swan," "Cries of London")	ARC 3053
Tomkins: *Musica Deo Sacra*	EA-27
―――― Songs and Consort Music	EA-28
―――― Church music ("When David Heard")	Van BG-604 (BGS-5031)
English Keyboard Music	EA-13
Byrd: Keyboard Music	Dec DL 10040
English Madrigals and Folk Songs	Angel 35461
English Madrigal School	Van BG-553,554,577
Morley: Canzonets, Madrigals, Ballads, Harpsichord pieces	ARC 3209
Elizabethan and Jacobean Ayres, Madrigals, and Dances	Dec DL 9406(79406)
Dowland: Lute Songs (including "Flow, My Tears")	EA-34, MHS 682
―――― Ayres for Four Voices	Argo RG 290
―――― First Book of Ayres (Five Voices)	Per SPL 727
―――― *Lachrymae, or Seven Teares*	EMS 12
English Lute Songs and Six *In nomines* (including Tomkins: *In nomine,* HAM, No. 176; Dowland, "What If I Never Speed," HAM, No. 163)	Van BG-576

bibliography

It would more than exceed the limits of available space to attempt here a list of even the most important works on the subjects mentioned in this book. The items given below are only a sampling of what the beginner in music history can find to supply additional information. Special attention is called to DucM, HeyHS, and SpHM, which provide a comprehensive roster of historical collections (*Denkmäler*), collected editions of the works of one composer, histories, biographies and so forth. Standard music dictionaries in English are Willi Apel's *Harvard Dictionary of Music* (Cambridge: Harvard University Press, 1946) and Westrup and Harrison's *The New College Encyclopedia of Music* (New York: W. W. Norton & Co., Inc., 1960).

COLLECTIONS OF MUSIC REFERRED TO IN THE TEXT

AM-E   Engel, H. (ed.), *The Sixteenth-Century Part-song in Italy, France, England, and Spain* (Anthology of Music), Cologne: Arno Volk-Verlag, 1961.

AM-F   Fellerer, Karl G. (ed.), *Preclassical Polyphony* (Anthology of Music), Cologne: Arno-Volk-Verlag, 1965.

AM-G   Gennrich, F. (ed.), *Troubadours, Trouvères, Minnesong and Mastersong* (Anthology of Music), Cologne: Arno Volk-Verlag, 1960.

AM-H   Husmann, Heinrich (ed.), *Medieval Polyphony* (Anthology of Music), Cologne: Arno Volk-Verlag, 1962.

AM-N   Noske, Frits (ed.), *The Solo Song Outside German-speaking Countries* (Anthology of Music), Cologne: Arno Volk-Verlag, 1958.

AM-T   Tack, Franz (ed.), *Gregorian Chant* (Anthology of Music), Cologne: Arno Volk-Verlag, 1960.

GlE   Gleason, Harold (ed.), *Examples of Music before 1400,* New
            York: Appleton-Century-Crofts, 1942.
HAM   Davison, Archibald T. and Apel, Willi (eds.), *Historical An-
            thology of Music,* Vol. I, rev. ed., Cambridge, Mass.:
            Harvard University Press, 1950.
ML   Hardy, Gordon and Fish, Arnold, *Music Literature,* Vol. II,
            Polyphony, New York: Dodd, Mead & Co., 1966.
Omn   Starr, William J. and Devine, George F. (eds.), *Music Scores
            Omnibus,* Vol. I, Englewood Cliffs, N. J.: Prentice-
            Hall, Inc., 1964.
P & O   Parrish, Carl and Ohl, John F. (eds.), *Masterpieces of Music
            before 1750,* New York: W. W. Norton & Co., Inc.,
            1951. (See Appendix for records belonging with this
            and ParT.)
ParT   Parrish, Carl (ed.), *A Treasury of Early Music,* New York:
            W. W. Norton & Co., Inc., 1958.
SteM   Stevens, Georgia (ed.), *Medieval and Renaissance Choral
            Music,* Boston: McLaughlin & Reilly Co., 1940.

                 BOOKS, ARTICLES, AND OTHER COLLECTIONS
AdI   Ady, Julia Mary, *Isabella d'Este, Marchioness of Mantua, 1474-
            1539,* London: J. Murray, 1932.
AnC   Anglés, Higini, *La Musica de las Cantigas de Santa Maria,*
            Barcelona: Biblioteca Central, 1943.
ApF   Apel, Willi (ed.), *French Secular Music of the Late Fourteenth
            Century,* Cambridge, Mass.: Medieval Academy of
            America, 1950.
ApG   —————, *Gregorian Chant,* Bloomington: University of Indiana
            Press, 1958.
ApN   —————, *The Notation of Polyphonic Music, 900-1600,* 5th ed.,
            Cambridge, Mass.: Medieval Academy of America. 1961.
ArO   Arbeau. Thoinot, *Orchésographie, et traicté en forme de dia-
            logue,* translated by M. S. Evans, New York: Kamin
            Dance Publishers, 1948.
AuC   Aubry, Pierre, *Cent motets du XIIIᵉ siècle,* 3 vols., Paris: Rouart,
            1908.
BaS   Baxter, J. H. (ed.), *An Old St. Andrews Music Book,* London:
            H. Milford. 1931.
BeK   Bedbrook, Gerald S., *Keyboard Music from the Middle Ages
            to the Baroque,* London: Macmillan & Co., 1949.
BesA   Bessaraboff, Nicholas, *Ancient European Musical Instruments,*
            Cambridge, Mass.: Harvard University Press, 1941.
BessM   Besseler, Heinrich, *Musik des Mittelalters und der Renais-
            sance,* Handbuch der Musikwissenschaft, Potsdam:
            Athenaion, 1931.
BlC   Blume, F. (ed.), *Das Chorwerk,* Wolfenbuttel: Moseler, 1929.
            This is a series of short volumes of music that includes
            many of the pieces discussed in the text in a form
            handy for study or performance.

BlR Blume, F., *Renaissance and Baroque Music,* translated by M. D. Herter Norton, New York: W. W. Norton & Co., Inc., 1967.

BraI Bragard, R. and de Han, F. J. (eds.), *Les Instruments de musique dans l'art et l'historie,* Brussels: Albert de Visscher, 1966.

BriV Bridgman, Nanie, *La Vie musicale au Quattrocento et jusqu'a la naissance du madrigal,* Paris: Gallimard, 1964.

BroA Brooks, Catherine V., "Antoine Busnois, Chanson Composer," *Journal of the American Musicological Society,* 6: III, 1953.

BuI Buchner, A., *Musical Instruments through the Ages,* translated by Iris Urwin, London: Spring Books, 1956(?)

BukM Bukofzer, Manfred, "The Music in the Old Hall Manuscript," *Musical Quarterly* 34:36, 1952.

BukS —————, *Studies in Medieval and Renaissance Music,* New York: W. W. Norton & Co., Inc., 1950.

BukU —————, "An Unknown Chansonnier of the Fifteenth Century," *Musical Quarterly* 28:14, 1942.

BusL Buszin, W. E., "Luther on Music," *Musical Quarterly* 32:80, 1946.

CaM Carpenter, Nan Cook, *Music in the Medieval and Renaissance Universities,* Norman: University of Oklahoma Press, 1958.

ChT Chaytor, H. J., *The Troubadours,* Cambridge: Cambridge University Press, 1912.

CoJ Collins, H. B., "John Taverner's Masses," *Music and Letters* 5:322, 1924, 6:314, 1925.

CoT —————, "Thomas Tallis," *Music and Letters* 10:152, 1929.

ColS Collison Morley, Lacy, *The Story of the Sforzas,* New York, E. P. Dutton, 1934.

CouM Coulton, G. G., *The Medieval Scene,* Cambridge: Cambridge University Press, 1930.

CrT Crocker, Richard L., "The Troping Hypothesis," *Musical Quarterly* 52:183, 1966.

CrosM Crosland, Jessie, *Medieval French Literature,* Oxford: Basil Blackwell, 1956.

CuC Cuyler, Louise E. (ed.), *The Choralis Constantinus Book III* (1555). Ann Arbor: University of Michigan Press, 1950.

DarP Dart, Thurston (ed.), *Parthenia In-Violata,* New York: C. F. Peters, 1961.

DavL Davis, William S., *Life on a Medieval Barony,* New York: Harper & Bros., 1923.

DiF Dittmer, Luther (ed.), *Facsimile Reproduction of the Manuscript Wolfenbüttel 1099* (1206), Brooklyn: Institute of Medieval Music, 1960.

DonI Donington, Robert, *Instruments of Music,* New York: Barnes and Noble, 1962.

DonO   Donington, Robert and Dart, Thurston, "The Origin of the In
              Nomine," *Music and Letters* 30:101, 1949.
DrT   Droz, E., Thibault, G. and Rokseth, Y. (eds.), *Trois Chanson-*
              niers français du XVe siècle, Paris, 1927.
DucM   Duckles, Vincent, *Music Reference and Research Materials*,
              London: Collier MacMillan, Ltd., 1964.
EaH   Easton, Stewart C., *The Heritage of the Past*, New York: Rine-
              hart & Co., 1955.
EinM   Einstein, Alfred, *The Italian Madrigal*, 3 vols, translated by H.
              Sessions and O. Strunk, Princeton: Princeton University
              Press, 1949.
FeH   Fellerer, Karl G., *The History of Catholic Church Music*, trans-
              lated by Rev. Francis A. Brunner, Baltimore: Helicon
              Press, Inc., 1961.
FelEC   Fellowes, E. H., *English Cathedral Music from Edward VI to*
              Edward VII, 2nd ed., London: Methuen & Co., Ltd.,
              1945.
FelEM   —————, *The English Madrigal Composers*, 2nd ed., Oxford:
              Oxford University Press, 1948.
FuV   Fuller-Maitland, J. A. and Squire, W. B. (eds.), *The Fitz-*
              william Virginal Book, 2 vols., reprint of 1899 edition,
              New York: Dover Publications, Inc., 1963.
GrB   Grant, Michael (ed.), *The Birth of Western Civilization*:
              Greece and Rome. New York: McGraw-Hill Book Com-
              pany, 1964.
GreD   Greenberg, Noah (ed.), *The Play of Daniel*, Oxford: Oxford
              University Press, 1960.
GuthG   Guthrie, William K. C., *The Greeks and Their Gods*, Boston:
              Beacon Press, 1951.
HarMB   Harrison, Frank Lloyd, *Music in Medieval Britain*, New York:
              Dover Publications, Inc., 1958.
HayR   Hay, Denys, *From Roman Empire to Renaissance Europe*, Lon-
              don: Methuen & Co., Ltd., 1953.
HelmS   Helmholtz, Hermann von, *On the Sensations of Tone*, trans-
              lated and edited by A. J. Ellis, Gloucester, Mass.: Peter
              Smith, 1954.
HewO   Hewitt, Helen (ed.), *Harmonice Musices Odhecaton A*, Cam-
              bridge: Medieval Academy of America, 1946.
HeyHS   Heyer, Anna H. (ed.), *Historical Sets, Collected Editions, and*
              Monuments of Music, Chicago: American Library Asso-
              ciation, 1957.
HoM   Hollman, Wilbur W. (ed.), *The Maastricht Easter Play*, New
              York: G. Schirmer, Inc., 1966.
HubT   Hubbard, Frank, *Three Centuries of Harpsichord Making*, Cam-
              bridge: Harvard University Press, 1965.
HuS   Hughes, Dom A., "Sixteenth Century Service Music," *Music*
              and Letters 5:145, 335, 1924.
IdJ   Idelsohn, A. Z., *Jewish Liturgy and Its Development*, New
              York: Sacred Music Press, 1932.

JaE   James, Philip, *Early Keyboard Instruments*, London: Holland Press, 1960.

JeC   Jeppesen, K., *Counterpoint: The Polyphonic Vocal Style of the Sixteenth Century*, translated by Glen Haydon, Englewood Cliffs, N. J.: Prentice-Hall, Inc., 1939.

JeP   ————, *The Style of Palestrina and the Dissonance*, 2nd English ed., London: G. Camberlege, 1946.

JuM   Jungmann, Joseph A., *The Mass of the Roman Rite: Its Origin and Development*, translated by Rev. Francis A. Brunner, New York: Benziger Brothers, Inc., 1951.

KeW   Kenney, Sylvia, *Walter Frye and the Contenance Angloise*, New Haven: Yale University Press, 1964.

KiP   Kinsky, Georg, *A History of Music in Pictures*, reprint of the 1929 ed., New York: Dover Publications, Inc., 1951.

KrüK Krüger, Walther, *Die authentische Klangform des primitiven Organum*, Kassel: Bärenreiter, 1958.

KuE   Kunst, Jaap, *Ethnomusicology*, The Hague: Nijhoff, 1959, with supplement, 1960.

LaB   Lang, Paul H. and Bettman, Otto L., *Pictorial History of Music*, New York: W. W. Norton & Co., Inc., 1960.

LiG   Lipphardt, Walther. *Die Geschichte des mehrstimmigen Proprium Missae*. Heidelberg: F. H. Kerle, 1950.

LU   Benedictines of Solesmes (eds.), *Liber Usualis, with Introduction and Rubrics in English*, Tournai: Desclée & Co., 1947.

MacM MacKinney, Loren C., *The Medieval World*, New York: Farrar & Rinehart, Inc., 1938.

MarD Marcuse, Sibyl, *Musical Instruments: A Comprehensive Dictionary*, Garden City, N.Y.: Doubleday & Co., Inc., 1964.

MariH Marix, Jeanne, *Histoire de la musique et des musiciens de la cour de Bourgogne sous le règne de Philippe le bon*, Strasbourg: Heitz, 1939.

MariM ————, *Les Musiciens de la cour de Bourgogne au XVe siècle (1420-1467)*, Paris, 1937.

MilG Miller, Walter, *Greece and the Greeks*, New York: The Macmillan Co., 1941.

MirD Mireaux, Émile, *Daily Life in the Time of Homer*, translated by Iris Sells, New York: The Macmillan Co., 1960.

MuC   Murray, Dom G., *The Choral Chants of the Mass*, Bristol: Burleigh Press, n.d.

MV   Benedictines of Solesmes (eds.), *Mass and Vespers*, Tournai: Desclée & Co., 1957.

NeM   Nettl, Bruno, *Music in Primitive Culture*, Cambridge: Harvard University Press, 1956.

NeT   ————, *Theory and Method in Ethnomusicology*, New York: The Macmillan Co., 1964.

NO   *New Oxford History of Music*, London: Oxford University Press, 1957-

PalMC   *Cantatorium of St. Gall, MS No. 359,* "Paléographie Musicale,"
            Series 2, Vol. II, Tournai: Desclée & Co., 1924.

PalMG   *Gradual de Bénévent, Codex VI.* 34, "Paléographie Musicale,"
            Vol. XV, Tournai: Desclée & Co., 1937.

Par   *Parthenia,* London: Chiswick Press, 1942.

ParN   Parrish, Carl, *The Notation of Medieval Music,* New York: W.
            W. Norton & Co., Inc., 1957.

PiH   Pincherle, Marc, *An Illustrated History of Music,* New York:
            Reynal & Co., Inc., 1959.

RamO   Ramsbotham, A., Collins, H. B. and Hughes, Dom A. (eds.),
            The Old Hall Manuscript, 3 vols. Burnham: Plainsong
            and Medieval Society, 1933-38.

ReMMA   Reese, Gustave, *Music in the Middle Ages,* New York: W. W.
            Norton & Co., Inc., 1940.

ReMR   —————, *Music in the Renaissance,* rev. ed. New York: W. W.
            Norton & Co., Inc., 1959.

RiE   Rice, Talbot (ed.), *The Dawn of European Civilization: The
            Dark Ages,* New York: McGraw-Hill Book Company,
            1965.

SaH   Sachs, Curt, *The History of Musical Instruments,* New York:
            W. W. Norton & Co., Inc., 1940.

SaRi   —————, *The Rise of Music in the Ancient World, East and
            West,* New York: W. W. Norton & Co., Inc., 1943.

SaWe   —————, *Wellsprings of Music,* New York: McGraw-Hill Book
            Company, 1965.

SaWH   —————,*World History of the Dance,* translated by Bessie
            Schönberg, New York: W. W. Norton & Co., Inc., 1937.

ScheM   Schevill, Ferdinand, *The Medici,* New York: Harcourt, Brace,
            1949.

SchlG   Schlesinger, Kathleen, *The Greek Aulos,* London: Methuen &
            Co., Ltd., 1939.

SchnO   Schneider, Marius, "Primitive Music," *New Oxford History of
            Music* 1:1, 1957.

SchrF   Schrade, Leo, "A Fourteenth-century Parody Mass," *Acta Mu-
            sicologica* 27:13, 1955.

SchrM   —————, "The Mass of Toulouse," *Revue Belge de Musicologie*
            8:84, 1954.

SchrMC   —————,*Monteverdi, the Creator of Modern Music,* New York,
            W. W. Norton & Co., Inc., 1950.

SchrP   —————, (ed), *Polyphonic Music of the Fourteenth Century,*
            4 vols., Monaco: Editions de l'Oiseau-Lyre, 1956.

SmH   Smith, Preserved, *A History of Modern Culture,* New York:
            Henry Holt, 1930.

SpC   Sparks, Edgar H., *Cantus Firmus in Mass and Motet 1420-1520,*
            Berkeley: University of California Press, 1963.

SpHM   Spiess, Lincoln B., *Historical Musicology,* Musicological Studies,
            No. 4, Brooklyn: Institute of Medieval Music, 1963.

StäF   Stäblein-Harder, Hanna (ed.), *Fourteenth-Century Mass Music
            in France,* Rome: American Institute of Musicology,
            1962.

StaM   Stainer, John, *Early Bodleian Music, Dufay and His Contemporaries*, London: Novello & Co., 1898.

StrS   Strunk, Oliver (ed.), *Source Readings in Music History*, New York: W. W. Norton & Co., Inc., 1950.

ThC   Thompson, James W., Rowley, George, Schevill, Ferdinand and Sarton, George, *The Civilization of the Renaissance*, Chicago: University of Chicago Press 1929.

ThoC   Thomson, James, *An Introduction to Philippe (?) Caron*, Musicological Studies, No. 9, Brooklyn: Institute of Mediaeval Music, 1964.

WadS   Waddell, Helen, *The Wandering Scholars*, Garden City, N.Y., Doubleday & Co., Inc., 1955.

WagM   Wagner, Peter, *Geschichte der Messe. I. Teil: bis 1600*, Leipzig: Breitkopf & Härtel, 1913; Repr. Hildesheim: Georg Olms Verlagsbuchhandlung, 1963.

WaiR   Waite, William, *The Rhythm of Twelfth-Century Polyphony*, New Haven: Yale University Press, 1954.

WeS   Werner, Eric, *The Sacred Bridge*, New York: Columbia University Press, 1956.

WerW   Wertheimer, Max, "Musik der Wedda," *Sammelbände der Internationalen Musikgesellschaft*, Jahrgang 2:300, 1909-1910.

WolE   Wooldridge, H. E. and Hughes, H. V. (eds.), *Early English Harmony from the Tenth to the Fifteenth Century*, London: B. Quaritch, 1897-1913.

YoD   Young, Karl, *The Drama of the Medieval Church*, 2 vols., Oxford: Oxford University Press, 1933.

index

(Page numbers in bold face refer to illustrations)

ELEMENTARY SCHOOL ADMINISTRATION:

READINGS